F O R E W O R
A U T H O R

REFINING
IDENTITY

I Am *Who* I AM *Says* I Am

COURTNEY COHEN

Refining Identity
I Am Who I AM Says I Am

by Courtney Cohen

copyright ©2013 by Courtney Cohen

Trade paperback ISBN: 9781942362036

Ebook ISBN: 9781942362029

Previous Trade paperback ISBN: 9781938624650

Cover design by Martijn van Tilborgh

Refining Identity is also available on Amazon Kindle, Barnes & Noble Nook, Google Play Books, and Apple iBooks.

Published by Now Found Publishing
Northlake, Texas
NowFoundPublishing.com

All scripture quotations, unless otherwise indicated are taken from the Holy Bible, English Standard Version, copyright 2001, by Crossway Bibles, a division of Good News Publishers.

CONTENTS

DEDICATION

To my husband, Steven, for seeing me how God does, always encouraging me to listen for God's voice and setting an example and standard in our home that is godly and trustworthy.

ACKNOWLEDGEMENTS

THIS BOOK HAS BEEN a nine-year-long journey for me, beginning with a simple outline God asked me to sketch out one afternoon. First and foremost, I want to thank Jesus, my Lord and my Savior, for His sacrifice and victory which allow me to set aside what culture tries to push on me as definitive and, instead take on Christ Himself to live in me, work through me and redefine me through and through. I am truly grateful and humbled to have been given this vision, calling and every resource to see *Refining Identity* come to pass.

Along the way, I have been blessed with dear friends who have prayed, encouraged, supported and given honest critiques to help me make this study all that it can be. Summer Hoover, Angel Mauldin, Carol Richardson and all my "Pink Life" ladies, you are priceless to me! Thank you will never be enough!

Gaye Moss, for teaching me about the "sweetness of God", thank you! Your own Bible studies have modeled to me a beautiful and user-friendly format which served as a great inspiration as I took a bunch of scattered thoughts and put them together.

Pastor Jan Greenwood, you blessed me so deeply with speaking a prophetic word over my life years ago, encouraging me as a communicator of God's words. Thank you for speaking into my life then and for continuing to reveal an enduring strength that is found only in Christ.

There were also several people who helped raise awareness for *Refining Identity*. Sian Smith, thank you for filming and editing a beautiful promotional video with such artistry and attention to detail! And, special thanks to Melody Fitzgerald, DT and Vanessa Frank, Angel Mauldin, Bethany Morical, Shelton and Carol Richardson Sr., Shelton Richardson Jr. and Michael and Jan Turner for your generous contributions.

To my amazing kids: Reece and Shelby, you are a daily reminder of my purposes and my identity found in Jesus. It is a blessing I cannot fully describe to be your mom and see you grow to know Jesus personally! Thank you for all your precious prayers for "Mommy's book". God has heard every one and He is faithful to answer.

And, to my husband, Steve, I want to say thank you for believing in me, backing me, uplifting me and encouraging me to always—and only—be the person God has created me to be. Thank you for setting an example of what it looks like to seek out God's approval alone and for stepping out in faith with me time and again to follow the steps God has laid out before us.

FOREWORD

SOMETIMES I THINK most of the earth's population is experiencing an identity crisis.

Our identity is so important. It not only defines the basics of who you are—like your name, or gender, or appearance—but so much more importantly, it helps us to understand how and where we fit into the world. Our identity sets us apart, goes before us into every new relationship and situation and ultimately has tremendous influence over how we feel about our purpose, our lives and ourselves.

As a pastor, I often find myself sitting face to face with women, listening to them struggle to feel valued, to find purpose, or even to understand or believe the character of our God. We are searching for acceptance and love—to be known. Sadly, our life circumstances or family dynamics often deposit some lies deep in our souls that, when full-grown, lead us to a sense of being unknown or unloved, essentially orphaned.

Just about the time we mature enough to begin to understand that there might be more to us than meets the eye, we simultaneously seem to lose a sense of our personal worth. We begin to measure ourselves by our performance or achievements, placing value on what we've done or what others think of us. Sometimes we even get so lost on this journey that we fight against our personal passions and waste our natural gifts. Tied up in the root of this problem is not just our confusion about ourselves, but ultimately a false view of our God.

No wonder we struggle to understand our true identity.

In *Refining Identity*, Courtney Cohen takes us on a discipleship journey that points us to the unconditional love of our Savior. Here we find all the answers to the questions we have about our true identity. Courtney leads us gently into places of revelation and safety so that we find the courage to define ourselves by the standard of our Creator rather than by the standard of our culture.

She uses the process of refining gold to illustrate how God works in our lives to separate truth from lies and to reveal the true, inner person inside each of us. Using her own life-story as a road map, she marks the way for many to follow. In her book, Courtney highlights the power of unconditional love and says, "God's love is proven by His sacrifice, His continual desire to pull us closer to Him and His ceaseless striving to purify us so that we may look just like His Son."

In getting to know Courtney as a friend and pastor, I discovered that she daily ministers hope and encouragement to others from the place of healing she herself experienced. Who she is flows naturally into her ministry and her writing. She doesn't just talk about these truths. She lives them.

Every page of *Refining Identity* is filled with easy-to-understand Biblical principles that you can apply. You will be encouraged to not just read about your identity, but to probe God's heart, search His Word for truth and discover for yourself the life-altering identity you can have in Jesus Christ.

Whether you are just beginning to look below the surface, or you are in the midst of your own identity crisis, Courtney will help you ask the right questions, look in the right locations and value the right perspectives in order to really know and love yourself.

Jan Greenwood
Pastor of Women, Gateway Church
Author of *Women at War*

INTRODUCTION

REFLECTING HIS GLORY

A<small>S A CHILD I LOVED FAIRY TALES</small> that involved a makeover of some sort. At the end of "Beauty and the Beast," the Beast was revealed to actually be the handsome prince in disguise all along. And, of course, the eternally classic Cinderella showed how an apparent nobody could be the most beautiful girl in the kingdom, valued above all others by the prince. Now, as an adult, I'm still a sucker for the makeover story. I love the before and after photos. This can range from a kitchen remodel to a house morphed from clutter-filled to organized and, of course, to the fashion makeovers that boost the confidence of men and women alike who are now ready to face the world.

Unfortunately, these makeovers, though uplifting in the moment and filled with encouraging ideas, lack the element that gives them lasting value. They highlight the desires of every human heart: to be better…to matter. But stopping there neglects the reason *why* these desires are within us all: **to reflect the glory of God.**

When a person realizes their need for Jesus to be his or her Savior, lifting up a faith-filled heart to Him as Lord, salvation takes place. That is a **singular** point in time. However, what theologians call *sanctification* is an **ongoing** process that takes a lifetime in which a person grows ever more into the image of Christ. In this earthly life, there is no one who has "arrived." Even our most admired teachers of the Word, the most devout servants of the poor, the most effective evangelists are still on their journeys towards becoming more like Christ. So, wherever you are on your path, take heart that you are not alone on this journey. And as you take each step in your life and trust God to lead you, you will find yourself reflecting His image more and more. This process of finding your identity in Christ is the best makeover of all!

I would like to offer a few words of warning as you look towards reflecting God in your life. First, open yourself up to what is here, and focus on how this might affect *you*, not another person you may know. Also, realize and accept that this is not a fast-fix. Set aside the desire for instant gratification. At the end of your time spent in this study, you will very likely not be completely wise and whole. But, you *will* be headed in the direction of God's will. You *will* have a better understanding of where your sense of worth comes from. And you *will* be better equipped to maintain that in a practical life setting. Finally, be truly open and honest not only with yourself, but especially with God, as you walk through this process and throughout your daily life. Only then will you be able to take on this identity of Christ as your very own.

When God first placed the vision of this book on my heart, I was a single woman, though in a committed courtship, living far from family and friends. My responsibilities were primarily only to myself. I had no one else I was responsible for or to answer to. Now, several years later, I am finally finished with writing this study, a vision no less diminished in my soul, though my circumstances outwardly are quite different. Now, I am married to the wonderful man I was courting. We have moved closer to friends and family, and we have two beautiful children. Life has been busy, insane at times, joyful, stressful, exciting, and for quite a while, even depressing.

Some of the very things I outlined in this book upon the first vision God gave me are those precise things that I have battled over the past several years. I have lost myself in my schoolwork, in my wedding plans, in my marriage, in motherhood to very young children, and in my work. I have allowed myself to slip away from knowing who I am in Christ. And this "slip" wasn't a brief period. It lasted three years. But, here I am on the other side. And God is to be praised because He has renewed my vision, confirmed my calling, and re-established my knowledge of my identity in Him!

I pray that this book is a blessing in your life. I pray that you will pore over the pages rather than skim through. I pray that if you are doing this study with others that you will truly give time and thought to it rather than rushing to finish your "homework" the night before your meeting. I am guilty of all of the above, but I know that God has a word to speak to your heart to heal you and bring you forth. Where you are now is **not** where He has destined for you to stay. We are not meant to be stagnant. We are to be ever moving forward towards His purpose, towards Him!

The way this study is designed to serve you is through purposeful interaction with the Word. You will absolutely miss the lessons within this book if you do not have your Bible sitting open next to you. I believe that you are seeking to hear from God. So I will, quite intentionally, not sum up the "correct answer" to every question. I want you to find the answers for yourself. There are questions to prompt your thinking and Scriptures for you to meditate on. I have found that, especially among evangelical Christians, silence, stillness, and Christian meditation are all but forgotten amidst our flurry of activity. I pray that we will all grow together in learning how to be still before Almighty God.

I hope to expose you to some scriptures that you perhaps have not come across before. I am certain I'll use some of the "classics" that you've already heard simply because they are excellent verses. But one goal I have is to challenge you to learn more of the Bible. The Word is our only offensive weapon against the attacks of the evil one. We must learn how to use it, and to do that, we must know what the Word says.

So, let's begin...

CHAPTER ONE

WHO IS THE REFINER?

"For who is God, but the Lord? And who is a rock, except our God?—the God who equipped me with strength..." Psalm 18:31-32

GOLD CAN BE REMOVED from the mine and purified to outstanding beauty, revealing such marvelous worth. But one thing is certain: *The gold cannot purify itself.* The Refiner is the One who takes the raw gold and transforms it into something stunning. He sees in the raw gold something most others wouldn't: the potentiality of what the gold will become. And He refines and refines, and the process continues over and again until the day comes when the Refiner looks into the liquid gold and sees His reflection. That is when He knows that the gold which once was raw has now become purified.

A Golden Truth:
God is the Refiner who transforms raw gold into pure.

Who is God? Could we start with a larger question? It is impossible to define who God is with any finality because He truly is beyond what our limited minds can conjure. But this study would be utterly wasteful if we didn't explore certain aspects of God's character.

God is not just some indescribable and powerful force out there. Yes, He is all-powerful, and yes, He is indescribable in all His fullness, but God is knowable in many ways. God is our Refiner. He deeply cares about us and wants to see us identify ourselves with Him through Jesus Christ. He is intimately involved in every aspect of our lives, whether we see Him or not.

What is your understanding about who God is? Will you take the time and opportunity to get to know Him with more intimacy and fullness?

How does Romans 8:17 define those who put their trust in Christ?

children of God / heirs of God &
co-heirs of Christ

We are co-heirs with Christ. Take a moment, and let that truly sink in. All that belongs to Christ is ours to share. If we are faithful to God amidst the victories and struggles of this life, we have everything to gain.

Read Genesis 1:27. As men and women, how were we modeled at the point of creation? What did God use as His blueprint when He decided to create humankind?

Himself

Why should you identify with God? *Why* should you find yourself in Him and through Him?

Because I am his child + heir & he made us in his image.

As creatures modeled after God, we are endowed with *His* splendor. Our words have power because *His* words do. We have wills to make choices in life. We have creative desires and abilities because those are aspects of *His* nature. We are evidence of *His* glory.

So, as we begin our journey into discovering who *we* are in Christ, let's look at a few traits of God and seek to better understand *first* who our Refiner is.

1) ALPHA & OMEGA

"From everlasting to everlasting you are God." Psalm 90:2

As I sit here writing today, I know I have only a few brief hours before I will need to pick up my kids from preschool. My day has limits within the confines of time. There is only so much I can accomplish given this limitation. My life had a clear beginning on the day I was born.

Time is no such constraint on God. In his classic book, *The Pursuit of God*, A.W. Tozer writes, "[God] is eternal. He antedates time and is wholly independent of it. Time began in Him and will end in Him. To it He pays no tribute and from it He suffers no change." (1)

What do the following verses reveal about God's relation to our/time?

Genesis 1:1   *Not sure*   "In the beginning"

Exodus 3:14 *I AM - present tense existence. I exist. (Outside of time)*

Psalm 90:1-4 *God exists beyond (+ before) time. From everlasting to everlasting you are God. Time w/ you is not marked as it is with us.*

Revelation 22:13 *God himself is the creator of time + the marker of its segments. He is the beginning + the end.*

God is self-existent. He always was and always will be, enduring forever and never changing. His name, "Yahweh," in Hebrew, literally means, "I AM." Who He was at creation is who He is today. Who He is today is who He will be tomorrow and in a thousand years.

How do the following verses show our relation to the eternal God?

Deuteronomy 33:26-27 *The eternal God is our dwelling place + we are in his everlasting arms.*

Isaiah 57:15 *God dwells with us at the same time as he dwells "in the high + holy place"*

It is challenging to imagine being free from the constraints of time. But this is how God dwells. He is the Source of all things as the Creator. He is the Beginning and the End, and He predates all beings and experiences. Though I am limited in my understanding of this ability to be separated in existence from time, I am comforted that my God is beyond such a thing. Something that constantly hems me in is nothing at all to Him!

2) TRINITARIAN & RELATIONAL

"Go therefore and make disciples of all nations, baptizing them in the name of the Father and of the Son and of the Holy Spirit." Matthew 28:19

Although the word "Trinity" does not occur anywhere in all of Scripture, the reality of that concept is found all over the place. The Trinity is a relational mystery. God is One, unified in substance and will, and yet is expressed through three Persons. Again, in attempting to understand an aspect of God's character, we have to remember that though we strive to comprehend, we are limited. But, despite these limitations within our minds' abilities to fully understand, it is still important to explore the evidence of the Trinity and see how that directly impacts our understanding of God.

God, existing in the Persons of the Father, the Son, and the Holy Spirit, is relationally complete. He did not create humankind because He was lonely and needed company. But in His ability to relate within Himself, He also desires to relate to you in a personal way.

How do the following verses reveal evidence for the existence of God in three Persons?

Genesis 1:26 *use of plural pronoun "our" "us"*

Matthew 3:16-17 *All 3 manifest @ same time: Jesus saw the Spirit of God which came to rest on him while God the Father spoke from heaven.*

Galatians 4:4-6 *God sent his Son* ① ② *God sent the Spirit of his Son.* ③

The first Person of the Trinity is the Father. God the Father sits enthroned in Heaven. He bears all authority. He is also called "Abba," which carries a similar meaning to the word we use, "Daddy." In recognizing God as our Father, or Abba, we begin to realize that He loves us as His own children.

What do the following scriptures reveal about God the Father?

Psalm 68:5 *Father of the fatherless → protector, protector of widows. He sides w/ the disenfranchised — these bullets*

Isaiah 6:1-4 *Absolute Ruler, enthroned in heaven. Set apart: Holy, holy, holy. Weightier than everything else in universe (glory). Awesome*

Ezekiel 1:26-28 *He is awesome beyond imagination. His appearance is beyond awe-inspiring: great brightness, fire, gleaming, blows you away*

Matthew 6:9 *His name is holy + should be hallowed - greatly reverend or reputed. Different than everything else.*

1 John 3:1 *Being called God's children show the kind of love He has for us. Full of steadfast love for us.*

The second Person of the Trinity is known by many names, but most commonly as the Son, or Jesus Christ. It is important to

GOD THE FATHER

John 10:10 The thief comes ~~to~~ only to steal + kill + destroy.

I am that they may have life + have it all

remember that although Jesus lived 33 years on earth as both fully man and fully God, He has existed for all eternity. Before Jesus lived on earth, He lived in Heaven. It is through this second Person of the Trinity that all of creation was called into existence. The Son is our Savior and Mediator before God the Father. As those who believe in Christ to save us from our sins and bring us into freedom, we can be confident that we are secure because of His sacrifice.

What names and qualities about God the Son are revealed in the following verses?

Isaiah 52:13 wisdom in actions, high + lifted up, exalted.

Isaiah 53:2-6 Nothing special to look at (no majesty, no good looks), despised by men, rejected, a man of sorrows, acquainted with grief. Carried our griefs + sorrows, pierced, crushed, chastised, wounded => for us, because of us

Matthew 1:23 born of a virgin He will be God with us. Emmanuel

Mark 6:4-6 a prophet - un-acknowledged or honored by those who knew him + his family.

Luke 19:10 His mission: he came to look for + rescue the lost. (seek + save)

John 1:1 / Revelation 19:13 He was the Word of God, existing forever with God + is God. Logos. Jesus' name is The Word of God

John 13:13-14

Modelled
Servanthood

Teacher
Lord

Acts 16:31 / Romans 10:9 / Colossians 2:6

our salvation - if we believe + confess
him. We receive Jesus as Lord
+ are to walk-live/follow him

1 Timothy 2:5

He is the one mediator
the btw us + God.

Hebrews 1:2-3

God sent Jesus to speak to us
Jesus is the heir of everything
God created the world thru Jesus.

1 John 1:7

Jesus is in the light - we are
to follow him — fellowship w each
other. His blood cleanses us from
sin.

The third Person of the Trinity is the Holy Spirit. Too often the Holy Spirit is minimized or altogether forgotten, but it is so important to remember Him and understand how He works in the lives of believers.

How do the following verses reveal the character and roles of the Holy Spirit?

Psalm 143:10

leads us

John 20:22   Holy Spirit   (involved in forgiveness?

Romans 5:5   God pours out his love thru the H.S. (that He gives us)

Romans 8:26   helps us in our weakness he intercedes for us (thank goodness!)

1 Corinthians 3:16

     God's spirit dwells in me

2 Timothy 1:14

     H.S. dwells in us.

1 John 5:6-7

     The Spirit testifies (that Jesus is the Son of God)

     to Jesus

Revelation 2:7

     The Spirit speaks to the church

And as important as it is to recognize the three Persons of God, it is also vital to remember that He is One, and not three separate beings. How do the following verses help us understand the unity of the Trinity?

Mark 12:29 *Jesus says The Lord is one.*

John 10:30 *I and the Father are one.*

I know that was a lot of Scripture to read through. The written Word of God is one of our best tools to help us understand the character of God. And God has been so good and gracious to us to help us see more of who He is and how He desires to relate to us in every moment.

3) WORTHY

"Let everything that has breath praise the Lord! Praise the Lord!"
Psalm 150:6

Any person attending a rock concert will easily see the praise being given: the voices from the audience singing along and shouting in affirmation, hands lifted toward the stage, people visibly overwhelmed by close proximity to the performers, even trying to touch an outstretched hand from the stage. Why?

Every person is hard-wired from the point of creation to be a worshipper. The problem that occurred at the Fall of Man, accounted in Genesis 3, is that the *object of worship* shifted away from the natural inclination towards God. In that act of disobedience and pride, God was removed from His proper place within the hearts of men and women. But the need to worship never diminished; it was only redirected.

In a world that lifts people up as "stars" and exalts possessions and titles, it is a hard thing, although a necessary one, to redirect our need to worship back to the only One who deserves it.

In the Shorter Catechism, we read in a few simple words the profound truth of the purpose of humankind: "*Question*: What is the chief end of man? *Answer*: Man's chief end is to glorify God and enjoy Him forever." (2) Only God alone is worthy of our worship, adoration, and praise. Yet, too often these are directed towards temporal things when they belong to Him only.

According to the Shorter Catechism, what is the bottom-line purpose in our lives as humans?

to glorify God

to enjoy Him

Read Ecclesiastes 12:13. How does this verse affirm the passage from the Shorter Catechism?

"fear God + keep his commandments, for this is the whole duty of man. If you fear Him + obey Him you are giving him glory."

What do the following verses reveal about *why* God alone is worthy of our praise?

2 Samuel 22:14-20 *He is our rescuer from strong enemies. He was my support*

Psalm 18:30

His way is perfect. His word proves true. He is a shield for all those who take refuge in him.

Psalm 139:14

His works are wonderful.
He made me.

The Psalms are teeming with praise for God, with so many descriptions of various forms of worshipping Him. How do the following scriptures show varying ways of worship?

Psalm 5:7 *enter his house, bow down*
in the fear of him

Psalm 9:1-2 *give thanks with whole heart*
retell his deeds. Be glad + exalt in
God. Sing praise to his name.

Psalm 17:3
to accept his testing
to purpose/decide my mouth
won't sin.

Psalm 33:1-3
Shout for joy. Give praise. Give
thanks w/ instruments. Make
Melodies, sing, & play + shout to God!

Psalm 34:1
bless the Lord all the time
his praise continually in
my mouth

Psalm 51:15-17
declare His praises
Sacrifices you like are a contrite
♡, broken spirit. Not burnt offerings

Psalm 149:3

Praise his name WITH DANCING
Make music to him w/ drums +
guitars .

From praising with our words, song, and dance, to playing instruments and going to the house of the Lord, to giving thanks, shouting for joy, and giving Him the sacrifices of our broken and contrite hearts, there are endless ways to praise Him. Psalm 149:4 says, *"The Lord takes pleasure in his people."* He loves to hear and witness our praise and adoration of Him. God created us for Himself, for His good pleasure. And our hearts will only find satisfaction when we place God back where He belongs: on the throne of our lives.

4) LOVING & JUST

"By this is love perfected with us, so that we may have confidence for the day of judgment, because as he is so also are we in this world."
1 John 4:17

The idea of *justice* is often incompletely considered to be equal to *punishment*. True justice is what happens when we receive the consequences of our actions, be they right or wrong.

A good parent, acting out of justice, will bless their child with praises and rewards for making good choices and obeying. That same parent will discipline their child for disobedience and making poor choices. These consequences teach children right from wrong and give them boundaries within which to live successfully.

This is what God does with us. He has established the boundaries. And for those of us who have made the choice to believe in His Son and trust in the salvation we receive from Christ, even our mistakes are covered by that sacrifice. All God can see when He looks at us is Jesus. So God *does* sit as Judge as He always has. But He has, Himself, *provided the payment* for our sins through Christ.

Another idea many of us struggle with is that it seems that those
who sin are not brought to justice. Usually this involves sins that
victimize others. But we have to remember that God's timeframe
is set apart from ours. He will be just because that is simply what
He is. However, often what we imagine as just is not how He will
carry out *His* perfect justice. We will spend more time later in this
study exploring sin, forgiveness, and healing. For now, let's focus
on God's pure love and faultless justice.

How do the following passages describe God?

Deuteronomy 32:4 *What he does is perfect all his ways are justice / just + fair. He is a God of faithfulness who sin - He does no wrong. Just + upright.*

Psalm 77:13 *His ways are holy. No one is like Him.*

There is no god like our God. In truth, there is no god that exists,
or has ever existed, other than our God, the God of Israel. But
even those things that are elevated in our world - those things
that are deemed praiseworthy - are nothing in comparison to
Him.

Read 1 Samuel 2:2-10. What will God do for those who depend
on Him? What will He do for those who reject Him?

guard + protect, *break them into pieces*

God stayed - did not forsake them

In Nehemiah 9:17-21, God exhibited love in several ways even
though His chosen people had repeatedly forsaken Him. How did
He love them? *Lead them clearly by day + by night, gave your good spirit to teach them, gave them food + drink,*

sustained them physically + spiritually.

Read Romans 3:21-26. How has God maintained His righteousness and saved humankind at the same time? How are sinners justified?

By having His Son pay the price— like the just punishment we deserve.

How do the following verses describe the love of God?

Psalm 103:13-14 *like the love of a dad for his children. He knows us— that we are dust. He's compassionate.*

1 John 4:16 *God loves us a lot. He is love.*

The love of God is lavished on His children. His justice is eternal. *"See what kind of love the Father has given to us, that we should be called the children of God; and so we are." (1 John 3:1)* **In God's love, He desired to adopt us. In His *justice*, He paid the price of adoption.**

5) EQUIPPING & DELIVERING

"And my God will supply every need of yours according to his riches in glory in Christ Jesus." Philippians 4:19

God's overwhelming desire to be intimately involved in the lives of His children can often be difficult to grasp. Perhaps we can accept that He loves us and has adopted us as His children. But it's harder to truly believe that God cares about the things in life that seem less "spiritual." Does He care if I need a mattress? Does He care if I need a computer to help me run my business? Does He care if my kids have outgrown their shoes and need new ones?

Let's take a look at the practical God we serve who equips those who love him. What do the following verses reveal about how God provides for needs?

Psalm 18:32

gives me strength

Are these the right verses?! I don't see how they answer the Q!

Psalm 18:33

makes me secure

Psalm 18:34

trains my hands for war?

God is the One who gives us the strength we need to do whatever tasks He sets before us. He can guide us, quite literally, in the steps we take and give us the knowledge and physical abilities that we need to face anything. Our role is to trust Him, obey as He guides, and give Him our all. He won't do the work for us. But He will give us every tool we require.

In 2 Timothy, Paul mentors a young evangelist, Timothy. He reminds Timothy of the calling placed on his life, encouraging him that God will provide exactly what he needs. Read 2 Timothy 1:6-7. What has God given Timothy? What has He *not* given him?

*gift of God
a spirit of power,
love +
self-control*

*a spirit of
fear*

Has God given you a calling for your life? If so, what is it? ✗ —

To love + serve him to love others.

I don't believe God has a "specific calling" —

Perhaps you have no idea what God's purpose is for your life. That's actually a wonderful thing to realize! Once you have considered this, you are on the road to caring more about what God wants for you than what you want for yourself. Then you can have an open spirit, ready to listen to Him.

What does James 1:5-6 say about asking for help? What will God give us? With what attitudes do we need to approach Him?

James 1 talks about asking God for wisdom. Attitude of faith not doubt.

How does Ecclesiastes 3:14-15 describe what God has done or will do?

It to Whatever God does endures forever - we can't △ it. He does "it" so that people will - have a right (reverent) view of Him - attitude toward him.

We can trust that every calling God gives will come to fulfillment if we are willing to walk with Him. Maybe it won't look like you thought it would. And, more than likely, the timing will be different than what you anticipated. But, never doubt that if He promised it and you obey Him in taking the steps He gives you, He will bring it to pass. If you need wisdom, He'll give it; if you need practical supplies, He'll provide; if you need time to hone your skills, He will help you see where that time can be found.

Now, one thing we need to remember is the difference between our needs and our wants. Often Philippians 4:13 is quoted out of context, giving the impression that if I wanted to be anything *I* desired, then God would strengthen me to do just that. It's convenient to ignore the previous two verses that shed light on the true meaning of Paul's statement, primarily because the reality of his situation is a bit uncomfortable to think about.

Read Philippians 4:11-13. When Paul wrote this, he was a prisoner. He had endured numerous physical beatings throughout his ministry (outlined in 2 Corinthians 11:24-33). What did Paul learn, regardless of any circumstance?

Paul has learned to be content regardless of his circumstances.
- He can do what is needed thru Christ who strengthens him.

What do the following verses reveal about the purpose of living in contentedness even during trying circumstances?

Proverbs 3:11-12

Discipline (from God) is a sign of God's love & fatherly concern & delight.

2 Corinthians 1:3-5

Father of mercies, God of all comfort God comforts us in affliction ⇒ We can give that comfort to others.

James 1:2-4 *Count trials joy - it is testing your faith which ⇒ endurance ⇒ perfect + complete, ⇒ lacking nothing*

Whether you currently live in abundance or in need, God is there and He sees. He will answer you when you call. He will show you as you come to Him in humility what your purpose is. And He will equip you to see that promise fulfilled. He is the Refiner. And as you seek to understand His will, He will refine you into ever-emerging purity, more and more able to live out your purpose. Part of that journey begins with discovering who you are. Now that we have taken a look at who He is, let's explore who He has made you to be.

REFLECTION...

Read each of the following names of God, and take some time on each one. Ask God to reveal to you more of His character. If you like, reference the Bible verses we've discussed earlier for more insight from His Word on who our Refiner is.

Alpha & Omega *Beginning + end "who is + who was + who is to come / the Almighty" the first + the last.*

Yahweh (I Am) *Always existing   the Great I am (let grace to say)*

Father / Abba *Jesus speaks to God this way; Abba, Father. sent Spirit of his Son into our hearts, crying, "Abba, Father."*

Ancient of Days (Daniel 7) *Name for God in Daniel 7. On the throne, judgment*

Teacher *- Rabbi (of Jesus) - one who instructs students / learners, One w/ answers + knowledge that others follow - to learn, listen to, become like.*

Lamb sacrifice
offering

Savior one who saves
Redeemer ~~of so~~ from sin
Saver of souls from death -
seperation from God

Servant
one who serves (no rights), who
performs duties for others

High Priest - goes into the Holy of Holies.
Can enter God's presence. Presents
people to God - acts on behalf of
men before God - offers sacrifice for
Helper their sins

- ~~one~~ one who assists, helps, gives aid

Guide - helping others to get to a destination,
Providing support, info + leading

Intercessor praying to God on behalf of
others

Counselor one who comes alongside
(paraclete) one who helps thru
wisdom, instruction

Read Psalm 18 completely through. Ask God to reveal to you how He is intimately involved in your daily life in providing for your needs.

CHAPTER TWO

GOLDEN...IN THE RAW

"For I will take you out of the nations; I will gather you from all the countries and bring you back into your own land...I will give you a new heart and put a new spirit in you..." Ezekiel 36:24, 26a

OUR SENSE OF WORTH and self-identity are so often wrapped around our assessment of how much we accomplish, the recognition of others, or feeling like we have somehow met the expectations we were "supposed" to fulfill. But, when we use these supposed expectations as our sole blueprint for our own self-worth, we neglect what God wants to work in us. No one is created to fit into a mold, especially one that has not been shaped by God.

God has endowed each of us with splendor and provided us with our own unique attributes. Beyond that, we were never intended to reach our potential through our own strength. At some point, if we truly desire to be the people God has created us to be, we have to be willing to hand over the controls, rip up our blueprints and allow Him to re-sketch our identities.

A Golden Truth:
We are gold. But in our raw states, we are hindered by our impurities.

"These [trials] have come so that your faith—of greater worth than gold, which perishes even though refined by fire—may be proved genuine and may result in praise, glory, and honor when Jesus Christ is revealed." 1 Peter 1:7

How does Peter compare the value of gold with the value of your faith in this verse?

Having greater worth than gold.

And just as with gold, we too must be refined. God turns up the heat in many ways. But this is only after we have realized that *He has accepted us just as we are*–golden…in the raw.

Before encountering Christ, we are all like gold in the rough, still held in place in a dark cave. But when we decide to surrender our lives to Him, we are pulled out of that cave, and the purification process is then able to begin. In order to allow God to refine us and to finally become who we are meant to be, the first step is to simply realize that what we are now is freshly mined gold, complete with dark impurities and hard spots. Do not lose heart with this image! This is a beautiful place to be! Remember that the God who saved you from the darkness is also the One capable of working change in your life.

1) DOING THE DO'S: OUR NEED FOR DEEDS

"For it is: Do and do, do and do, rule on rule, rule on rule: a little here a little there." Isaiah 28:10

"Doing the do's," means going through life as though it is a checklist. This can occur on a daily basis, or even over the course of a lifetime. Is there a part of your life that you micromanage because of a need for control?

Not sure. I make lists + schedule in order to keep up w/ demands of work + household.

In this verse, Isaiah the prophet was speaking to the people of Ephraim who had become highly legalistic in their ways of life. A self-imposed need for deeds caused them to become weary, but they refused God's available resting place and instead kept on in their mindset, assured that deeds were the way to righteousness. *"So then, the word of the Lord to them will become: Do and do, do and do, rule on rule, rule on rule; a little here, a little there— so that they will go and fall backward, be injured and snared and captured." (Isaiah 28:13)* This image isn't exactly a comforting one. The people of Ephraim allowed the Word of God, our written source of guidance and an expression of His undying love for us, to become a harsh and cold to-do list.

Read Hosea 8:7. *"Sow the wind" won't harvest results of their labor*

By taking on too much, more than we can truly handle, and especially by putting our faith in those deeds, those circumstances, we "sow the wind." We plant something that cannot last and that we cannot maintain. We place our focus on the futile things that this world embraces. And therefore, we "reap the whirlwind." We experience resulting overwhelm and poor performance in life. We can experience depression, confusion, and burnout. We simply do not understand why, during this time, those things that the world embraces did not fulfill or maintain us.

What do the following verses reveal about things that people hide behind?

Amos 4:4 *Religious practices (tithing, offerings) being public in their religiosity/rituals*

2 Thessalonians 3:11

[handwritten] being busy about other people's lives (instead avoiding doing your own work)

?

God is not impressed by our offerings of money or time if we first do not offer Him our hearts. *Is there something that you are hiding behind?*

[handwritten] ?

Read Philippians 2:12.

These words seem to indicate that our job is to work *for* our own salvation…that our salvation is *dependent* upon things that we do. This, however, is a grossly misunderstood verse simply because we do not continue to read.

Read Philippians 2:13. *Why* does God work *in* us?

[handwritten] to will + to work for his good pleasure.

[handwritten] getting things done (to earn God's approval) => the giving of self.

Yes, following Christ requires work. But one absolutely vital concept we too often fail to grasp is that *God gives us the ability to do whatever work He deems worthy of doing.* He does not leave us high and dry to fend for ourselves. He gives us every tool we need.

When my heart focused on getting things done in order to earn God's love, I became enormously unforgiving of myself. I realized one day that I had been holding my sins over my head for years, allowing them to keep me in a handicapped and unproductive state of being. We will discuss this more later on, but for now, we need to understand that by holding grudges against ourselves we are only hindering the beautiful cleansing rain of forgiveness that God so desperately desires to pour over us. We are only maintaining barricades between who we *used to be* and who God *wills us to be*.

2) PRIDE AND SELF-DEPENDENCE

"When I surveyed all that my hands had done and what I had toiled to achieve, everything was meaningless, a chasing after the wind; nothing was gained under the sun." Ecclesiastes 2:11

King Solomon intimately knew of the worthlessness of focusing on personal achievement. When our emphases are self-focused or on seeking personal gain, we are headed in the wrong direction. In fact, we are going in the opposite direction of God's intent, because self-focus leads to pride and robs God of His due glory.

Read Ezekiel 28:17 and Genesis 3:2-6.

Pride was central to Satan's fall from heaven. Pride led to the fall of mankind. And pride is an immense part of what keeps us distanced from God. Our enemy promises fulfillment through anything other than Christ. And he entices us to become the gods of our own worlds. In our quests for self-sustenance and individualism, we take on the false perceptions that we should be able to come into our own, on our own. We become wise in our own eyes.

A Personal Note...

In those rushed moments, just before leaving the house to head to church, I took charge of readying our then 8-month-old daughter while my husband dressed our 2-year-old son. First, my son appeared in a shirt and shorts that, while both blue, simply didn't match. After I voiced my objection, my husband changed our son's clothes. When my son emerged again, I saw that he wore a sleeveless shirt, more suited for playing sports than attending church in my opinion, and a pair of shorts. We were already running late, but still, I went and grabbed a collared shirt and matching shorts, still casual, but much more "put together." After this little episode, my husband asked me why this mattered so much. Why, week after week, day after day for that matter, do I want my entire family to look a certain way at any given event? Well, that's just what you do. You don't show up to church looking like a slob when you have clothes in the closet that look more appropriate. You give God your best! But my husband saw through this weak ideology. I, on the other hand, had never taken the time to probe this line of reasoning. This was just how life was. But over the next hour, I came to realize that the issue actually was my desire for others to look well upon me. If my kids show up well dressed, that reflects well upon me as their mom. But if they show up mismatched or sloppy, that speaks to anyone who cares to notice that I can't manage my family well. We were obviously too rushed to take the time to dress decently. I obviously must have wasted time or not have been appropriately prepared. Perhaps I was lazy and had forgotten to do the laundry for a week or two. So, through one outfit on my 2-year-old son, I thought I communicated to the world that I was a bad mom, non-punctual, lazy, uncouth, and a terrible homemaker. Wow! See how the spiral goes around when pride takes control?

(margin, handwritten, vertical) What is my identity wrapped up in?

Read Galatians 6:3-4. How does this verse contrast the pride God gives with the pride that comes from comparing oneself to others?

(handwritten) deceptive
no one else is responsible
for my "load"

This God-given pride means that a person can take joy in knowing that he or she is in the will of God. This is confidence, not arrogance. In this confidence, we do not compare ourselves with anyone else. We no longer need to base our personal worth on some sort of a rating scale using worldly standards. God is our standard. He is the only one we need.

Read 2 Timothy 1:7. What is the difference between self-discipline and self-dependence?

(handwritten) In the former, I work hard at self-control to bring/keep myself in line w/ God's ways + desires.
Self-dependence - I rely on me to make it. Don't look to God or others; ignore the interdependence of the body.

Self-dependence and self-discipline are often confused. Self-dependence is reliance upon oneself for strength and sustenance. Self-discipline, rather, is reliance upon God to provide us with the needed strength and sustenance to do whatever it is that we have been called to do. A self-disciplined person then takes those provisions and applies them in a way which glorifies God, not self!

What do the following verses reveal about how, and who, God equips?

Deuteronomy 31:7-8 *God goes before them. He is with them. He won't leave or forsake them.*

Psalm 18:31-39 *God equips us w/ strength, gives + makes us in the way we need to be; makes the way for us to go (wide place, strength)*

1 Corinthians 1:26-31 *Those who are foolish in the world's eyes weak, low + despised things that are not*

2 Corinthians 12:6-10 *When I am weak - God can work in + through me + all will know it is God + not me, so He will receive the glory due his name.*

From our human perspectives, power means we must achieve perfection and control without revealing weaknesses. But God's view, on the other hand, is that *our* weaknesses are God's perfect opportunities to reveal *His* power through us.

God is an *equipping* God. He makes sure that those who trust in Him have the tools to move through the challenges of life. However,

He never intends that we should strike out on our own. He beckons us to His side and promises fulfillment as we obey Him.

3) DOING THE DO'S BY OTHERS' STANDARDS

"Am I now trying to win the approval of men, or of God? Or am I trying to please men? If I were still trying to please men, I would not be a servant of Christ." Galatians 1:10

Before accepting Christ into his life, Paul was a Pharisee, intently focused on maintaining righteousness through the Law. His life centered on keeping up appearances and persecuting Christ-followers, who affirmed that salvation was a gift of grace, which severely inhibited his attempt to gain God's favor through the Law. But Paul's focus shifted dramatically upon meeting Jesus. His adamancy transferred over to living a life of faith. His focus was no longer on obeying the Law in order to gain God's love. Rather, he accepted God's love, knowing he was a sinner, which enabled him to lead a life of example. The opinions of others no longer mattered. *"As for those who seemed to be important—whatever they were makes no difference to me; God does not judge by external appearance." (Gal. 2:6)* God's opinion was the only one by which Paul sought to abide.

Why do we strive to people-please? Many times it is tied to a desire for recognition. Our senses of worth are equated with the levels of pleasure others take in us. People-pleasing is also driven by fear. We want desperately to keep the peace and avoid rocking the boat because a part of us is afraid to lose these people. But there is a massive difference between honoring, respecting, and loving those around us and attempting to appease them out of fear.

Read Genesis 28:6-9.

In this section of Scripture, we see the obedience of Jacob contrasted with the people-pleasing of his brother, Esau. Back in Genesis 27:46, Esau and Jacob's mother, Rebekah, was speaking to her husband,

Not accurate (

Isaac, about how difficult Esau's wives made her life. When Jacob made a wise decision to follow his parent's guidance in seeking a wife, he received his parents' blessing. This caused jealousy to stir in Esau, which led him to people-please. And this landed him in an even messier situation. Now, he had three wives to juggle, and he still lacked the blessings of his parents and of God!

As Christians, we have obligations to follow God's path, regardless of the circumstances. We are called to love and serve others. We are *not* called to depend on others to give us our senses of worth or to follow others when it leads us to stray from living in the will of God. A painful, but eventually wonderful byproduct of following God's path is that it will pull us, and those in our immediate vicinity, out of our comfort zones. When we allow ourselves to be stretched beyond our comfort zones, we rely more upon God and less upon ourselves and others. And He is able to grow and strengthen us, ultimately expanding our territories of comfort.

Read Romans 1:24-25. What does this verse say about the consequences of serving the creature rather than the Creator?

God gives them up to their own sinful desires.

We must choose: Do we serve what God *created,* or do we serve *God?* Part of the problem in doing the do's is that we place others' opinions on a pedestal, accepting that their beliefs are superior to our own and, more tragically, superior to God's. To be sure, there is a need for wise counsel. But when, for every decision, we seek out twenty opinions on the matter, we are left flailing, with no ability to sift through all the information.

People pleasers also tend to think that the world has much more interest in them than what is actually true. They think that somehow they are central to ridicule and discussion. And because people pleasers live according to this belief, they live in a constant attempt to look like they know what they are doing. This is actually a form of pride–pride lived out of fear. It is very likely that most people we think are analyzing and critiquing us aren't even aware we are in the room. Worrying and fretting over how to appeal to everyone is a losing and purposeless battle.

Read Psalm 27:10. How does this verse contrast receiving acceptance from people and God?

> *Though my father + mother forsake me, the LORD will receive me.*

How do the following verses reveal the promises of God's faithfulness?

Lamentations 3:22-25 *His blessed love. It never ends, nor do his mercies. Each day they are new because of his great faithfulness. He is what we need - our portion/provision.*

2 Thessalonians 3:3 *The Lord is faithful + he will strengthen + protect you from Satan.*

God is truly faithful, and He gives a sure foundation on which to build. People-pleasing, regardless of our methods or motives, leads to a roller-coaster effect for our self-concept, actions, preferences, and decisions as we move all over to please and appease. As those we conform to shift, so do we. We lack foundation and assurance. We have no idea where to seek God's will or what it might look like. This is why Paul encourages us to *"not conform any longer to the pattern of this world, but be transformed by the renewing of your mind. Then you will be able to test and approve what God's will is— his good, pleasing and perfect will." (Romans 12:2)*

We can only know what God wants for us when we are no longer overcome with what others think we should do.

4) FILLING UP THE EMPTINESS

"Therefore we do not lose heart. Though outwardly we are wasting away, yet inwardly we are being renewed day by day. For our light and momentary troubles are achieving for us an eternal glory that far outweighs them all. So we fix our eyes not on what is seen, but on what is unseen. For what is seen is temporary, but what is unseen is eternal." 2 Corinthians 4:16-18

A Personal Note...

One evening while I was in college, I went to my church's singles' ministry. This was a regular, weekly occurrence of mine for several years. This particular time, though, I came in with a bizarre and indefinable sense of oppression. Although I was "doing well" - classes were great, I was in a wonderful and godly relationship, I was heavily involved in a women's ministry, my family was well, and everything else seemed to be in place - I felt incredibly low and on the verge of tears the entire evening. As a cordiality common to social gatherings, many people came up to me and asked, "How're you doing?" And of course, they really didn't want to know. They just wanted to make sure I knew that they had acknowledged my presence, so they would feel free to move on. After all, you can't be close friends with everyone. My repetitious and completely false reply was a simple, "I'm fine. How're you?" as we passed one another and avoided prolonged eye contact that would obligate further discussion. With each of these dozen or so pseudo-dialogues, I became more and more depressed and hurt. I imagined what these people would say or do if I actually told them that my heart was broken for some unknown reason. How would they react if I just let the tears flow, and I allowed myself to scream out of my frustration? Finally, I reached my last straw, thankfully, with a young woman who was more than a simple acquaintance. She asked me, "How're you doing?" And I replied, "My stats are great, but I am broken inside, and I don't know why." The tears began to form in the corners of my eyes. She truly was a Godsend at that moment, because she pulled me aside, with genuine care and interest and exhibited to me what a true sister-in-Christ does. She cared enough to listen.

Have you ever felt completely empty, as though you had nothing else to give? And yet you wondered, "This can't be happening, everything is so perfect in life, I should be happy." Perhaps your "stats" are great...but inwardly you feel like you are dying. What causes this emptiness? While there can be many initial causes, misplaced dependency and the search for self-worth apart from God are typically influential factors.

There exists a false and destructive assumption that godly people do not struggle or deal with weaknesses. We all have our struggles, and we all have our areas of weakness. But these are not failing points! These are opportunities to allow God to shine through us. You don't have to continue living behind a veil, hiding who you truly are. Even our weaknesses can be areas where God uses us most!

The problem is that we do not embrace our weaknesses as we should. Part of the human design is a built-in need for God. This need, this yearning, is an intentional aspect of God's creation. While He gives us free will to choose what path we walk, *"He has...set eternity in the hearts of men; yet they cannot fathom what God has done from beginning to end." (Ecclesiastes 3:11)* We know with inner, often indescribable knowledge that there is something beyond ourselves. Why else do people spend so much time and effort seeking to answer the question: "What is the meaning of life?" It's because we have a built-in drive causing us to ask this question that leads us to God. This inner desire draws us to God, but only by our free will can we come to Him and accept Him.

However, when people choose to ignore Him, that need does not just conveniently disappear. It is there to stay as conviction, evidence of God's ardent hope that we will someday turn towards Him. So, when we do not allow God to fill that void, we feel a vast emptiness, an unquenchable thirst. And no substitutes will suffice. Those tangible things such as romance, food, a job, wealth, accomplishment, and so forth simply lose their luster. They may mask the desire for a little while, but it comes back full force and eventually reveals the pointlessness of pursuing these any longer. *"Whoever loves money never has money enough; whoever loves wealth is never satisfied with his income. This too is meaningless."* *(Ecclesiastes 5:10)*

Whatever thing we want apart from God, we will never have enough of. God is the only thing that is more than enough.

What do the following verses reveal about our contentedness and how it relates to our dependency upon God?

Psalm 103:5 [the LORD] who satisfies you with good so that your youth is renewed like the eagles's.
God satisfies us w/ good => renews our vigor.

Proverbs 15:16 Better is a little w/ fear of the LORD than great treasure + trouble w/ it.

Proverbs 17:1 Better is a dry morsel w/ quiet than a house full of feasting w/ strife.
conflict, bitter disagreemnt.
leaning, relying on stuff doesn't bring Peace

Philippians 3:7-11 Indeed I count everything as loss because of the surpassing worth of knowing C. Jesus my Lord. ...that I may know him + the power of his resurrectn, + may be share his sufferings, becoming like him in his death, that by any means possible I may attain the resurrctn from the dead.

Philippians 4:11-13 Paul learned contentment in any circumstance based on doing all things thru Christ who gives him strength.

Everyone experiences limitations, even the most sincere and adamant followers of Christ. Paul, who wrote approximately one-third of the New Testament and who is one of the most influential teachers the Christian faith has ever known, expressed weakness that allowed God's strength to be revealed.

Read 2 Corinthians 12:7-10. What is an area of weakness in your life where you must rely upon God to give you His grace and strength? *Controlling my tongue*

- *mental health*
- *Working efficiently*

I know what it is to run from my weaknesses. But I also know what it is to have my weaknesses covered over by God's graceful strength. Suddenly those things that I thought hindered my walk, my testimony, and my effectiveness become brilliant and bright additions to every aspect of my existence and my influence. God is seen most clearly in those moments when I admit that I am weak, and I submit my will to His.

Read James 1:23-24. *Look carefully into the perfect law that sets you free AND DO WHAT IT SAYS (+ don't forget it)* Recognizing our weaknesses for what they are can often be frightening experiences. The Word of God has a tendency to point out what we have neglected in our lives. There are two ways of responding to viewing something unpleasant when looking at the mirror: disgust and shame OR acceptance and purpose to change.

We work so hard on the temporal things of this world, as though they had eternal significance. Often, these things are terms by which we measure ourselves and our personal levels of success. I call these my "stats" as you saw earlier in this section. And those things of eternal significance, we put off until "we have time," which often means they are put off indefinitely.

What does Psalm 39:4-7 say about our lives on earth?

Oh LORD, make me know my end + what is the measure of my days; let me know how fleeting I am! Our life span is a breath-fleeting, short. We spend our lives doing things that will disappear, be forgotten, so we won't keep them.

David expressed in these verses how he longed to have a greater knowledge of where value in life dwelled. He realized that chasing after temporal things in this life is hugely futile when compared to the fact that existence beyond this "breath" is eternal. That *eternal existence* is where our focus needs to be.

Death is a part of life - a doorway that separates this brief time we have on Earth from eternity. It will happen. Therefore, in our time here, we need to invest in the eternal rather than panic over what we can or cannot have in the present. *And in focusing on the eternal, the emptiness of the present drifts away.*

5) DOING THE DO'S VERSUS WHAT CHRIST HAS ALREADY DONE

"...If righteousness could be gained through the law, Christ died for nothing!" Galatians 2:21

Part of the problem with pride is that it assumes that righteousness can and is supposed to be achieved through good deeds of personal accomplishment. We get so bogged down by our flailing attempts to grasp holiness and righteousness because we think that God is inaccessible if we still have dark spots and impurities.

Read Luke 15:18-20.

In the parable of the prodigal son, after going off arrogantly, gallivanting, and wasting away a fortune, the son returns home humbled. This is Christ's illustration of God's love and salvation for us: God is our Father who is waiting for us to turn from our prideful directions and head His way. And in His loving-kindness, He comes *to us,* He reaches out *to us,* He makes up huge parts of the distances we need to travel. We just have to face Him and walk towards Him.

God will reach us where we are and walk the rest of the way with us!

What do the following verses reveal about the source of our confidence and righteousness?

Psalm 5:7 *thru the abundance of your steadfast love ~ I will enter your house*

Romans 5:6-9 *while we were still weak Christ died for us sinners. God pardoned us - by paying the cost/price - while we were not righteous. His blood justifies us He saves us from the wrath that we deserve!*

2 Corinthians 3:4-5 *Our sufficiency is from God - our confidence too. Not qualified on our own - comes from God.*

One precious gift we have through salvation in Christ is confidence. We gain confidence to live, to approach God in prayer, and to walk in God's will. No amount of our so-called righteous deeds will ever gain us this confidence. Only by accepting this gracious gift can we walk through life securely.

Part of our human design is a built-in need for God. One aspect of allowing Him to fill this void is to take sober stock of what Christ has done for us because, if we continue doing the do's, we neglect what Christ has already done! And if we ever hope to have the emptiness filled, we must turn toward His direction and trust that He will guide us the rest of the way! We have to admit our need for God's standard to be our **only** standard!

What does Philippians 3:12-14 say about reaching for perfection?

It seems to say he keeps going to reach for perfection. It's Goal

?

We are each uniquely designed, tailor-made for God's purposes. And any life other than the one He has created for each of us will simply never fulfill. Our clarity and solutions will never come from within! They only come from one source, and that is Jesus Christ! Whether you are trying to win favor in the eyes of your family or friends ...whether you are trying to please another person or yourself...as long as your focus is on these things for purpose and worth, you will never find them!

A Personal Note...

At 19 years of age, I sat down and penned a universal question we all seek to answer: "Who am I?" Although I had accepted Christ before this point, I was still living an empty life. My life was stuck in a cycle of trying to please others and prove to them my "goodness" or "capability." When I finally came to a humbled realization that none of these things gave me what God could give, I abandoned those pursuits, and started to learn what it meant to seek after God and His kingdom. But one of the most profound aspects of that moment was that despite all the ugliness of my past, I was able to repent and receive God's complete forgiveness. He still saw me as His child, useful for His purpose, and beautiful to behold.

It is an amazing paradox that someone can do such horrible things, yet those things still do not define who they are! A child of God chooses to be defined by something else, by something very different. He or she chooses to be defined by something not even of him or herself, but by the identity of Another, of Jesus Christ. God calls each of us to sacrifice things, to nail them to the Cross, and turn from them. While this may be excruciatingly difficult for us, in the end He hands us something immeasurably better - life to the fullest!

than the dust we are pursuing

REFLECTION...

Filling that emptiness and finding our completeness, and ultimately our refined identities in Him, is a journey. It is a process. Our first step in this process is just to accept where we are. *See* the impurities and the weak spots and *accept* them. The longer we deny them the greater a burden they will become. Also realize that there are very likely weaknesses we are currently unable to see. As we pray and seek God's perspective, He will make these areas clearer to us.

This journey requires choosing God over self. God, in His infinite wisdom, has designed us this way: Our thoughts lead to our emotions, and our emotions lead, ultimately, to our actions. This is why we can *"demolish arguments and every pretension that sets itself up against the knowledge of God, and we take captive every thought to make it obedient to Christ." (2 Corinthians 10:5)* In doing this, we allow God to "renew our minds" as Paul urges in Romans 12:2. Then, our emotions and actions can follow in suit.

Too often we give our emotions free reign in our decision-making. We need to become aware of this and realize that our emotions should not control us. Rather, the will of God expressed to our renewed minds will be a guide for our emotions, our actions, and therefore, our life decisions when we allow Him access to our lives.

As we will also see in the following chapters, in order for this present lump of impure gold to be refined, it must endure the fire. Do you have a tendency to feel the fire and jump out for fear of pain or decimation? I challenge you to walk through this fire of challenges and trials because God has an identity for you that you cannot even comprehend at this moment. And if you allow the refining process to continue, He will purify you to become a direct reflection of Christ!

Read Ezekiel 36:24-27.

Ask God to take you out of "the nations," which are your dependencies on yourself and anything aside from Him. Ask Him to redefine you as you seek your identity in Him.

CHAPTER THREE

BROKEN AND SURRENDERING

"The sacrifices of God are a broken spirit; a broken and contrite heart, O God, you will not despise." Psalm 51:17

IN THE PROCESS OF REFINING GOLD, the next step can be quite painful. Just as a hammer slams against a hunk of impure gold and breaks it into more manageable pieces, so do we seem to be hit and broken into scattered pieces. Where we thought we once had it all put together, or at least we looked solid on the outside, we realize now that *we were actually one solid mess that needed to be broken.* Our pure identities found in Christ will never come about as long as we remain in our solid clump, impurities and all. We must submit ourselves to be recast, remolded, and remade into what our golden element was intended for.

A Golden Truth:
Purification begins with brokenness.

A Personal Note...

Several times I have envisioned myself encapsulated in a hard cover of my own creation. This cover that I'd meant for protection made me cold, un-emotive, distanced, and depressed. But I was afraid that letting go of it would cause me to fall apart. I've imagined what would happen if I allowed God to remove this protection I'd created. I saw myself huddled in a ball, bleeding, and helpless. But then the most amazing thing happened. I saw God come to me and gently bind all my wounds. He allowed me to bleed so that I would know that I need Him. And then He came and put me together again. He is my Healer.

Read Psalm 51:8-12, 17. What do these verses reveal about the sacrifice God truly desires?

A broken spirit
a contrite heart (or broken)
^ feeling remorse or guilt
repentant ♡

This psalm is so vitally important to the message of this chapter. God does not seek out perfect people to follow Him. He calls those who are imperfect and weak. He desires us despite our impurities. Yet He also requires that we trust Him, surrendering our impurities to His control. This psalm cries out for cleansing and purification. David, in writing this psalm, acknowledges his own personal sin and filth. He admits his need and becomes wholly dependent upon God. This psalm speaks of complete and utter surrender to God. Therefore, we must come to God with honesty and willingness. Then we will be open for God to refine us into pure gold.

In this section, we will first look at the starting place for finding our true identities. Be honest with yourself and with God. Take a good look at where you are and why you may at times get frustrated, try to control, or feel helpless. When you look in the mirror, what do you see?

1) HONEST & WILLING

David was bold, poetic, and strong. He appealed to both men and women because of these characteristics as well as his love of God.

He was even called *a man after God's own heart* (1 Samuel 13:14). But he was not without his failings. David wrote Psalm 51 right after Nathan the prophet confronted him with his sins of adultery and murder. This psalm is nothing if it is not a picture of naked honesty before God. David was brutally honest with God. We hear his ups and downs throughout the psalms as he soberly assesses his circumstances and faithfully acknowledges God's supremacy.

Read Psalm 38:9-10. How often are you this honest with God? Where do you turn *first* when you aren't sure what your next step should be? All the time.

I often go to Tom or else other family to talk thru next steps.

We looked at pride, dependency on self and others, and resulting emptiness in the previous chapter. Now that we see the failings of these paths and our desperate need for God, the sanctification of Christ, and the guidance of the Holy Spirit in our lives, we must set aside all sense of show and be willing to stand naked, opening up sight of every blemish and imperfection to God. Nothing will ever change or improve in our lives until we are willing to take this challenging step. We must openly say to God, *"Search me, O God, and know my heart; test me and know my anxious thoughts. See if there is any offensive way in me and lead me in the way everlasting."* (Ps 139: 23-24)

Being honest and willing before God means that the attitude of our hearts is, *"I cannot have genuine and lasting change in my life apart from God!"*

God has given us the incredible blessing of free will. And practically from the dawn of time, we have misused it. As we seek to understand who we are in Christ, two things are certain:

He *will not* come in to change us without our invitation, and He *cannot* change us if we are dishonest.

Read the following verses. What do these people have in common?

Genesis 12:1, 4

Abram obeyed God. (So Abram went as the LORD told him.."

Judges 4:4-9 *Deborah + Barak - God told Barak to fight + he did (w/ Deb)*

Ruth 1:15-18 *Could not be dissuaded from staying w/ Naomi, following her... willing to go*

A person useful to the work God is doing is a person willing to make the journey, however long and however difficult. Abraham, Deborah and Ruth, along with countless others, made this journey in their own times.

With what attitudes are we to communicate with God?

Ecclesiastes 5:1-7 *Ready to listen; NOT talking promptly obeying; Don't make promises unless you are going to keep them.*

Matthew 6:7-13 *Don't keep babbling + blithering God knows my needs - pray w/ God in mind: He is in heaven, he's holy, he rules*

With an honest and willing heart, we must communicate with God, sharing with Him our thoughts and struggles and waiting to hear from Him in return. God is not looking for pious words. He is not impressed with your "Thee's" and "Thou's." He wants to know that your heart is broken when you feel you cannot communicate with your spouse. He wants you to share with him how desperate you feel about your challenges in disciplining your toddler. He wants to hear from you when you don't know where the next paycheck is coming from. Of course He already knows what is on your heart, on your mind. But as in every successful relationship, there must be communication.

Once we clearly see that we've allowed our identities in the past to be formed by something or someone other than Christ, and we release that bondage, there are empty spaces that need to be filled. We cannot remain stagnant and stop with acceptance of our current state of being. We must press on and discover our true selves – who God would have us become.

2) COURAGE TO FACE HIDDEN WEAKNESSES

"Have I not commanded you? Be strong and courageous. Do not be frightened, and do not be dismayed, for the Lord your God is with you wherever you go." Joshua 1:9

I have often wondered why the same message was given to Joshua repeatedly–not to be afraid but to be strong and courageous. (See Deuteronomy 3:21-22, Deuteronomy 31:7-8, and Joshua 1:8). He is reminded time and again by Moses and then by the Lord, directly, that God is with him wherever he goes, so he has no need to fear. I can only think from this repetition that perhaps Joshua dealt with some uncertainty in his ability to lead after having been led by Moses. Perhaps he considered himself too weak and under-qualified to hold such an honored and weighty responsibility.

It's amazing to me that God didn't simply give up on Joshua or any of the people who at first doubted their abilities to follow His calling. And so, over time, through various battles, Joshua obeyed and began to trust in God's faithfulness to lead even someone like him. He did not allow fear of the unknown to hinder his calling and movement forward in obedience. That is true courage.

Courage is not the *absence* of fear. **Courage, instead, is acting in obedience to God *despite* fearful opposition**. Courage is a vital element needed to power this ongoing process of refinement toward our identities in Christ. We all have areas of weakness, and these are opportunities to choose whether we will continue to be run by our fears of having to face those weak points or whether we will allow courage to face them head on, preparing the way for change.

What do the following verses say about God's ability to see, reveal, and heal what is hidden?

Psalm 139:11-12 *If I say, 'Surely the darkness will cover me' Even the darkness is not dark to you ... for darkness is as light with you.*

Daniel 2:22 *he reveals deep + hidden things, he knows what is in the darkness*

1 John 1:6-9 *If I confess my sins, he is faithful + just to forgive my sins + to cleanse me from all unrighteousness.*

This journey is for the bold. Our habitual sins, whether we're aware of their presence or not, must be surrendered. David had the courage to ask God to explore his soul intimately and point out the offenses. He told God to test him, to know his heart, and then to lead him *"in the way everlasting." (Psalm 139:23-24)*

We all can list certain things about ourselves that we know are our weaknesses. And, yes, we need to give those to God to heal, mold, reshape, and bind up. But beyond what we already know, there is a very good chance there are issues in our lives we are unaware of, which hold us back from living lives that reflect God and His purpose.

What do the following verses reveal about the *purpose* of being cleansed from our hidden sins and weaknesses?

Philippians 1:20 *to honor Christ*

2 Timothy 2:20-22 *to be a vessel for God's use "set apart as holy, useful to the master of the house, ready for every good work"*

A Personal Note...

When a couple gets married, they usually exchange words like "...For better or for worse, in sickness and in health, for richer or poorer, till death do us part." That couple stands before God and commits to the long haul, regardless of the circumstances, despite the fact that they truly don't know what's around the corner. Eight days after our wedding, for example, Steve was in surgery. That wasn't in our plan, nor were the next six weeks of recovery for him while I bore the burden of moving us from Texas to Colorado. We had the immediate challenge - and privilege - to put our vows to the test as we remained vulnerable to each other. It's like that with God. When I surrendered my life fully to Jesus, something in me cried out for what I didn't have on my own: the peace, love, and acceptance that only comes from a relationship with Him. So I made a commitment to Christ. And that was not a one-time commitment - just as marriage isn't. I must continuously open myself up more and more to Him to tweak those things I wasn't aware of previously. In marriage, we stay committed regardless of that death in the family, regardless of the unexpected medical bills, regardless of the financial strain. We stay committed, or we fail the covenant we made. We stay committed with God to continue to unfold our hearts before Him regardless of the discomfort in the moment, regardless of the uncertainty. We stay committed to God, the source of our identities, or we lose the very identities we were trying to find on our own.

How do the following verses show us how we are to open ourselves up to God with courage?

Psalm 31:24

2 Corinthians 13:5

Examine
test yourself

Waiting to hear from God is something we must become accustomed to. If we rush through prayers and fail to listen to Him, we miss out on what He longs to share. So, ask God what things you do or burdens you may carry that you are unaware of. Ask Him to search you, test you, and lead you through this process of refining your identity with Christ.

Read Joshua 7:1, 10-26

This story of Achan is rich with lessons and courage, vulnerability and failings, and, of course, quite a few controversial feelings for those of us reading. It's not an easy story to deal with, but I believe that it well-suits this idea of finding courage to face hidden weaknesses that we must address.

For generations, especially after the death of Moses, Israel failed in keeping her covenant with Yahweh. Time and again, they accepted and worshipped the gods of the pagan people living in their midst. I've often thought how weak they must have been to do such a thing after having witnessed the daily miracles of God. But then, I look at how easily I can do the same thing in my own life. No, I don't physically bow down to a small statue of a false god, but I have, many times, bowed my heart to the things that the world cherishes. There is no difference in what I have done and what Israel did.

However, Joshua and the people of Israel showed incredible courage to face the hidden weaknesses within their people who were meant to be a light to the world revealing God's provision, power, and standards.

Achan disobeyed the will and order of God by *coveting* and *stealing* things that God had ordered to be devoted to Himself, either by burning or by putting in His treasury. However, Achan took those things: a beautiful cloak, silver, and gold, and *buried* them in the ground within his own tent.

Because of this disobedience, Israel lost the covering and favor of the Lord. Read Joshua 7:12 again. How was Israel to regain the Lord's favor?

destroy the devoted things

I can only imagine how painful this process was to bring Israel near by tribe, then clan, then family, then man-by-man knowing that the end would be someone's death. Purification from this sin, this hidden weakness, could only be achieved through shed blood.

For those of us who have received Christ's sacrifice on our behalf have been spared our own spiritual death, but we have to always remember that blood was indeed shed...Jesus' blood. Our sins, our hidden weaknesses, could only be purified through a perfect sacrifice.

We will only be cleansed from those sins when we place them under the authority of that sacrifice made for us. But laying those sins down requires that we first face them, acknowledge their existence, and then ask God to help us extract them from our lives.

Read Psalm 139:23-24. How would you describe David's attitude in this question?

The attitude must be: I don't care what it takes! We have to want *Him* more than we want whatever it is we're trying to hide.

3) VULNERABILITY BEFORE GOD

"The Lord is good, a stronghold in the day of trouble; he knows those who take refuge in him." Nahum 1:7

If you consider the idea of vulnerability, there are quite a few meanings. One is to be in danger, unshielded, and susceptible to harm. Another meaning is to be exposed and to be dependent on someone or something outside of oneself. It is the latter definition I want us to grasp in our search for vulnerability before God.

Read Psalm 44:20-21. What does this verse tell you about our ability to hide from God?

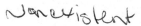

Oftentimes, it seems easier to live believing that God is so distant that He doesn't *really* see all that encompasses us, that He isn't aware of our flaws. It is a vulnerable thing to realize that this is simply not true and that in order to find peace and joy, we must open ourselves up to God, allowing Him to pick us apart and put us back together in His timing, with His purpose. Again, here we must choose courage over fear. Let the desire of each heart be: **I want to be known by God!**

Let's take a look at the story of Esther to see what vulnerability looks like. As a bit of background, Esther was a young Jewish woman living in Persia during a time of exile for the Israelites. The king deposed his wife, Queen Vashti, due to her refusal to parade her beauty before the king's court at his request. Then, he began the search for a new queen to take Vashti's place. So every beautiful, young virgin was taken, often by force, as a candidate.

Read Esther 2:8-14.

By outward appearances, Esther's position appears horrendous: an orphan, kidnapped from the only family she knows; a Jew who must hide her true heritage for fear of being killed; a virgin about to be suffered to lose her innocence to appease a king; and a woman who will spend the rest of her days in a harem without hope of ever having a husband or family. It seems as though she has no control over her set of circumstances and no hope for the future.

Read Esther 2:15-17. To whom does Esther make herself vulnerable? Why? *The Eunuch in charge of the harem.*

The king's eunuch, Hegai, who had charge over the women, had insider information as to what would please the king. If Esther had any hope of a future, she must be chosen as queen. Otherwise, she would merely be a castoff left to rot in the king's harem. Esther chose wisely to depend on Hegai. She could not trust her own judgment since she did not know what the king desired. Her vulnerability to the eunuch proved a wise move, and she gained favor, pleased the king, and was crowned the Queen of Persia.

In Esther chapters 3 and 4, the story continues. Haman, the king's second in command, had a murderous hatred of the Jews. He plotted to kill all the Jews in Persia and convinced the king to give his seal of approval, which Haman used to affirm the order to kill. Esther was positioned in such a way that she was the only one who might gain the king's favor to save the Jews from a massacre. Though she still lived in secret regarding her heritage, she needed to come forward, approach the king, and make Haman's evil intent known, which would expose her true identity as well. But, in the custom of the day, any person to approach the king without having been summoned could be immediately executed, even the queen! The only way to be saved from such a fate was if the king extended his scepter to that person. Anyone approaching without invitation was totally at the mercy of the king.

Read Esther 5:1-3. How did the king respond?

Esther later told the king about Haman's intent to kill the Jews across all of Persia. In her vulnerability, she had gained the favor of the king and was given his approval to allow the Jews to defend themselves. The Jews were victorious and were saved by Esther's bravery through her vulnerability to the king, despite frightening circumstances. Though she could not control her set of circumstances, she could control how she handled them. She had to be vulnerable or witness the massacre of her people.

In her vulnerability to Hegai, Esther was saved. Through her vulnerability before the king, the Persian Jews were saved!

What do the following verses reveal about what results from being known by God?

Job 23:10   *I shall come forth as gold.*

Psalm 91:9-10   *protection*

2 Timothy 2:19   *God knows those who are his — they must turn from evil.*

4) DEATH TO SELF

"I have been crucified with Christ. It is no longer I who live, but Christ who lives in me." Galatians 2:20

A Personal Note...

The pre-teen years are usually the awkward ones for most people. As for me, I had glasses, unruly, mousy hair, and no sense of style. Combined with my bookish and shy personality, I was often made fun of or simply ignored altogether. Even though I've grown older and learned the usefulness of contacts and hair products, I'm still bookish and somewhat reserved when around new people. But I hardly resemble that awkward twelve-year-old I once was. Nevertheless, it's so easy to still think of myself as awkward even after all these years have passed. Sometimes I can still see myself as who I used to be rather than who I have become. And that's merely taking into account the physical traits and personality quirks. How much more tempting is it to rely on the picture in my head of who I was before Christ took over my life than to allow that picture to die and live in the freedom He always intended?

The pinnacle of vulnerability before God is reached when a person realizes that he or she is helplessly alone. When Christ was crucified, it was not only our damning sins that were obliterated. It was also our flesh, our natural sin, our self-focus and selfishness, our intents, purposes, and personal agendas. In order to fully receive the miracle of what Jesus did for us on the cross, we must let go of what we have allowed ourselves to be defined by for so long.

We must make a choice about what is important: our sense of pseudo-control over a façade of an identity or something greater... God, who longs to recreate us, mold us, and work through us.

What do the following verses say about our righteousness and behaviors apart from God?

Philippians 3:8-10 *All our stuff is trash - rather desire to obtain the righteousness that comes thru faith in Christ — it comes from God — depends on faith*

Titus 3:3 *on my own, I'm a slave to my passions + pleasures, full of evil + envy + hating others.*

God has no need for us to impress Him with our righteous deeds. He just wants our love and trust. Countless lives have been changed and have changed the course of history because people who thought they were weak surrendered their identities to God and allowed Him to work through them.

Moses lacked eloquence and self-confidence. But God worked through him to free the Israelites from Egyptian oppression and lead them to the Promised Land (Exodus 4:10-12). *Joshua* was merely a son of Moses' aide and had to be constantly reminded not to be afraid. But he led the Israelites into even more battles and victories than Moses, leading them to conquer and finally take a hold of the Promised Land (Joshua 1:1-9). *Mary*, the mother of

Jesus, was seemingly small and unimportant, but she released that identity to allow the purpose of God to flow through her. And through the least likely source, God brought His Messiah to save the world (Luke 1:35-38, 46-49).

The apostle *Paul*, when he was called Saul prior to his conversion, thought his righteousness defined and justified him. But he laid that down for Christ's righteousness, which was the only one that could last and be truly worthy of the holiness of God (Philippians 3:3-9).

What do these verses reveal about our hope in Christ's death? What has God promised to those who believe and receive Jesus' sacrifice?

Colossians 1:21 (22) *God has reconciled me - I was his enemy - separated from God by my evil thoughts + actions. But God reconciles me to him thru the death of Jesus. ⇒ He brings me into his presence. He makes me holy +*

2 Timothy 2:11 *blameless - He makes me stand before Him w/o a single fault. If I have died w/ him, I will also live w/ him.*

Read Ezekiel 36:26-36. What promises does God give to those who surrender themselves to Him? Why does He do this? *ourselves God promised Israel a new tender heart + filling with His Spirit so they will follow his commands. He promises a homeland + an identity as God's people, cleansing from sin, blessings, provision. God does it to reveal Himself to*

It is amazing that God takes what is dead and worthless and replaces it with life and holiness! Whether people are seemingly small and unimportant or they think themselves full of self-righteousness that will save them, all are nothing next to His standards of holiness. Whether it is shame or pride, fear or weaknesses, release them all to God, and find new life in Him with the death of your old self.

the surrounding nations.

5) CHOOSING GOD'S WILL OVER OUR OWN

"Your kingdom come, your will be done, on earth as it is in heaven."
Matthew 6:10

Read Joshua 24:14-15.

If this passage of Scripture had been written today, perhaps it might have looked something like this: *"Now, therefore fear the Lord and serve him in sincerity and in faithfulness. Put away your trust in your financial portfolio and the range of your skills in trade. And if it is evil in your eyes to serve the Lord, choose this day whom you will serve, whether your clothes or house, your bank account or job title. But as for me and my house, we will serve the Lord."*

Those who have died to themselves will ask for God's will to be done rather than their own. They will say to God, "We are Yours." They understand that money can give no true and lasting security, that it can disappear in an instant. They understand that prestige, among other forms of flattery, is fleeting and depends upon how easily they bend their wills to others. Choosing to trust in God rather than the things of this world does not often lead to popularity among those who live as the world does. But it is the only true security and lasting satisfaction in this life and the next.

What do the following verses reveal about the power of your will to provide your own security?

Job 1:20-22

No matter what I achieve or amass in this world, I came in with nothing, + I go out with nothing. God is in control.

Romans 7:15-25

I can't even do what I know to be right! And what I know is wrong, I keep doing. W/ my flesh I serve the law of sin.

Galatians 2:21

Christ had to die because I cannot help make myself right w/ God apart from His grace.

Read Psalm 121. How does the Lord help you?

He watches over me - shades me. Keeps me from harm. He watches over my life + he never sleeps. He keeps me from losing my footing.

Read Job 23:12-14, and spend a quiet moment considering this passage. Have you *"treasured the words of his mouth more than your portion of food"*? If not, are you prepared to do so?

Sometimes - or I should say - at times. Not consistently.

Do you trust that God will complete what He has appointed for your life, even *"many such things"* beyond what you can imagine?

I don't think Job is talking about good things here (decrees against me) I am terrified

I guess so.

Read Matthew 26:39-42. What <u>attitude</u> can we learn from Jesus' model during this heart-wrenching moment in time?

Asking w/ acceptance
Nevertheless your will be done
Please X, but if not, your will be done.

We are at a point of decision. Perhaps you have believed in Jesus' sacrifice and are sure of your salvation. But have you handed over the controls to Him? Who will you allow to *guide* your life? Will you allow God, who knows you more intimately than you could ever hope to know yourself, to have this role? In this process of life and seeking out Christ's identity to come to life in you, a battle between your will and His will be a pressure revisited time and time again. It is an ongoing choice to submit. Make it.

REFLECTION...

A Personal Note...

I've often wondered why I get so easily flustered when things don't go exactly the way I planned. One of my personality hurdles is the tendency to judge myself harshly. I somehow think I am supposed to be Superwoman...able to do it all! And I am crushed when I realize, each and every time, that this assumption is completely wrong. Writing this study, over the course of several years, has forced me to deal with some of my most challenging issues. The evil one whispers in my ear, "What good can you be to anyone while you're still struggling with these things?" But truthfully, what good would I be to anyone if I had never struggled with my identity and if it wasn't still a constant struggle in my life? Where does the circle of frustration even begin? It all begins when I try to take control.

Gold that remains in its original lump cannot reflect the face of the Refiner. *"Neither is new wine put into old wineskins. If it is, the skins burst and the wine is spilled and the skins are destroyed. But new wine is put into fresh wineskins, and so both are preserved."* (Matthew 9:17)

As you are honest and willing, open and vulnerable to God, ready to surrender and receive His will, your old identity will be broken; so be prepared for new and unimaginable experiences and purposes for His glory. Those things on which you have previously depended must be broken off. They hold no value and are unable to prepare you for the calling God has for you.

Read Psalm 139.

Ask God to impress upon you the depth with which He is involved in your life. Ask Him to "search [you]...and know [your] heart...try [you] and know [your] thoughts...see if there be any grievous way in [you], and lead [you] in the way everlasting!"

ongoing choice to submit to God's will.

CHAPTER FOUR

MELTING THE FALSE IDENTITY

"And we all with unveiled face, beholding the glory of the Lord, are being transformed into the same image from one degree of glory to another..." 2 Corinthians 3:18

ONCE THE MASS OF GOLD has been broken up, those pieces are placed in a pot over a fire. The fire liquefies the pieces, and the liquid begins to boil.

As the heat turns up on our spiritual lives, the pretense of the identities we've portrayed up to this point becomes more apparent. We become more aware of imperfections that are based in our selfish ways. After coming into relationship with God, we feel the tension between the dark ways of our pasts, and the light, which are the ways God is leading us towards. It is truly a time of surrendering to the flame of God's will.

A Golden Truth:
God's fire will melt away the false identities we've hidden behind for so long.

When we repent and receive forgiveness, we begin to exchange our perspectives for God's. When sins are left unconfessed in your life, they will keep you restricted with a sense of separation from God and unable to see yourself rightly. God, through Christ, has provided a secure path out of the mire of our sins. But first, we must recognize their presence and surrender them to our Refiner.

1) REPENTANCE & GOD'S FORGIVENESS OF SINS

"I said, 'I will confess my transgressions to the Lord,' and you forgave the iniquity of my sin." Psalm 32:5b

One of the most wonderful passages explaining the need for repentance and the graciousness of the Lord's forgiveness is David's Psalm 32. He walks us through his experience in being bogged down in his sin, realizing his need to repent, confessing to the Lord, and receiving God's forgiveness and guidance as he moved forward in his life. And, as is characteristic of his psalms, David ends the passage with praise for God. I love how David reveals such practicality in this text, showing the reader the *consequences of unconfessed sin* and the *blessings of forgiveness.*

Read Psalm 32 completely through. How do you relate to David in his explanation of being "dried up" due to being silent and refusing to confess? Are there unconfessed sins in your life that are bringing you down and sapping your strength?

I always have sin to confess. From lack of kindness & forbearance to swearing + hopelessness.

What is promised to those who love God and confess their sins to Him?

forgiveness
a place of shelter
deliverance
instruction

Repentance, as David laid out in this amazing psalm, is first acknowledging the presence of sin rather than hiding it, confessing that sin to the Lord, changing our minds about that sin, and willfully turning away from that sin in our lives. God, in response to David's confession, said, *"I will instruct you and teach you in the way you should go." (Psalm 32:8a)* It is not enough to confess only. We must turn away and seek God's perfect path. Then we are assured of God's blessing on our lives and that we will be made into people "upright in heart."

What do the following verses reveal about God's promise to forgive?

2 Chronicles 7:14 When we humble ourselves pray, seek God's face, turn from wicked ways — then God hears + forgives + heals.

Ephesians 1:7 I am redeemed by his blood forgiven of my sins due to abundance of his grace

1 John 1:9 If we confess our sins, he is faithful + just to forgive us our sins + clean us from all unrighteousness.

Often this can be difficult because our sin is founded in habits. We are used to certain behaviors or attitudes, and it is a struggle to change. And, in truth, as long as we rely only upon our own strength and willpower to change, we will fail. It is only when we humble ourselves before God and seek His face that we will be able to see lasting change take place.

Read Jeremiah 31:31-34. This passage of scripture outlines a promise that we can now experience through the sacrifice made by Jesus Christ. What promises does God give?

that we will know him + his laws will be written on our hearts. + he'll forget our sins

What do the following scriptures show about *why* God forgives?

Psalm 130:3-4 *Not sure, If he didn't no one would survive, His forgiveness → a fear/awe of God.*

1 John 2:12 *for the sake of his name*

It has grown to be an unpalatable idea to think too much about the blood of Christ. We sum it up nicely and cleanly, without too much mess and discomfort to describe the means of our salvation as attributable to "the cross" or "Jesus' sacrifice." Rarely do we really dwell on the actual blood He shed for us. I would guess that at least in some part this has to do with our lack of understanding of Old Testament culture. It's easy to be disgusted by reading about thousands upon thousands of animal sacrifices outlined there. Often, we simply skim over their mention, trying hard not to picture how the Israelites slit the throats of the animals and poured out the blood on the altar, red and dripping down, even splashing on the tunics of the priests offering up the sacrifice. It's unnerving to take the time and think about it because it is so distant from what we are culturally accustomed to.

Read Hebrews 9:22. Why was the shedding of blood necessary? *Required for forgiveness of sins Sort of payment/cost.*

How does Hebrews 9:12-14 reveal how and why Christ's blood was shed? *Fulfilled Law of God - Jesus entered into Holy of Holies by Jesus w/ his own sacrificial blood - which paid eternally*

Read Romans 5:1, 9. How can we know that we have been forgiven?

by faith in what Jesus accomplished I have been justified by Jesus' blood which saves me from God's wrath that my sins deserve

We must constantly allow that process of purification from our sins to live on as we give them up to Him. Then we must let our sin go, just as the old saying goes, "Let go, and let God." When we let a sin go, we remove its power to define us.

2) FORGIVING YOURSELF

"Then I shall be blameless, and innocent of great transgression."
Psalm 19:13b

It's one thing to recognize the sin in our lives and confess it to God and then receive His forgiveness. It is quite another step altogether to purposefully forgive ourselves. Children of God should not so severely punish themselves, and yet they often do. We need to see the truth about the source of our condemnation and realize that it is not coming from the God who has extended His forgiveness.

A Personal Note…

I asked Christ to be Lord of my life when I was a mere five years old. And, having grown up in a Christian home, I learned all the right things to say and all the terminology of a "good" Southern Baptist. But in hindsight, I can see that although my salvation was secure in that precious moment, it took another fourteen years before I truly owned my own faith rather than piggybacking off my parents' faith. So, during my teenage years and first year of college, I allowed peer pressure and my low self-esteem to be my guides rather than Jesus. In and out of ungodly relationships, I sold myself short time and again. God used an unexpected meeting with a perfect stranger to shake me up quite a bit and help me realize the sin that I was walking in. Over the next few months, I made major adjustments in my life and sought God's forgiveness of my many sins. But, deep inside, I still carried a burden. I still thought of myself as dirty. I thought the shame of my sinful choices was mine to bear as a lifetime consequence. Quite simply, I hadn't forgiven myself.

I truly adore the way that David spoke to God in his psalms. I love his honesty and humility before the Almighty. There's no doubt that David made quite a few mistakes in his life, the most memorable being his adulterous affair with Bathsheba and the murder of her husband he committed afterwards. He also failed to raise up his sons from his other wives in the way of the Lord. It's wonderful for me to see so many of his failings and still know that God identified David as a man after the Lord's heart. Part of that is because David acknowledged when he sinned, and he then repented. His identity also stemmed from his trust that God's forgiveness of his sins meant that he could then be considered blameless and innocent. *He learned how to forgive himself by believing more in God's promise than in the condemnation within his heart.*

Read Psalm 19:12-14. What does this passage reveal about the results of God's forgiveness? What was David's confidence here? What was he sure of?

What do the following verses reveal about *how* and *why* we are able to release the sins of our past?

Romans 6:6-14

Philippians 3:12-14

1 John 3:18-20

A Personal Note...

I remember one day, August 19, 2001, to be specific, I was sitting at home and I felt restless. The silence of my bedroom was overwhelming, and I thought I'd go crazy if I didn't get out. So, I grabbed my things and raced out the door. Driving in my blue VW bug on familiar roads, God spoke directly into my heart. He told me I needed to forgive myself because He already had. Realization swept over me that I was carrying a burden I wasn't supposed to carry! And the tears began to stream. I probably should have pulled over since the tears blurred my vision...there are the hindsight and wisdom of being a bit older. I made it safely, by the grace of God alone, to my favorite coffee shop and managed to mop up my tears well enough. Once I settled with my coffee and a journal, I wrote the question that ended up being the basis of this very study, "Who am I?" Two weeks passed, and I hardly stopped writing in that time. I'd never journaled so much in my life! And in all that writing God began telling me who I was according to Him. I still get goose bumps thinking of that time in my life, remembering the divine healing that took place within my heart. He cleansed me! He defined me! I was dirty no more. My shame was gone, and I knew that Jesus had finally taken His proper place as Lord of my life.

I had been holding onto my past sins and allowing the enemy to continuously remind me of my failings. Reminders can come from anywhere if we allow them: people who know our past, places we used to go, gifts or pictures that remind us of those people from former, sinful relationships. Part of letting go after we've received God's forgiveness is asking Him if there are possessions we hold onto that are binding us to our sins through our memories. Allow Him to guide you to those things, pictures, and so forth that you need to toss out.

Read Micah 7:18-19. What do these verses reveal about God's memory of our confessed sins?

God has this amazing ability to forget sins. He simply chooses to throw them away into the sea of forgetfulness, and they are gone forever. We, on the other hand, struggle to truly forget things of the past. Many things we will never forget. And the enemy of our souls capitalizes on this by constantly reminding us of our failings. This is where we need to renew our minds with God's Word. (Romans 12:2)

Read Romans 8:31-39. What message does this passage convey about God's forgiveness and the forgiveness we can then grant ourselves?

The enemy cannot bring charges against us and force us to live in perpetual shame of our pasts if we choose to trust that God is for us. God is the one who justifies. Our thoughts and memories, the tauntings of the evil one, the people from our past...none of these things have any power over us that *we do not allow.* Instead of living forever in this bondage, choose to let go of whatever it is that burdens you. Once God has forgiven us, how dare we hold onto something that inhibits our usefulness for His glory! Holding onto sin leads to depression, low self-esteem, and self-hatred that have no place in the lives of His children! Believe in God's forgiveness, and trust that He has forgotten your confessed sins.

3) HIGH-RISK PRAYERS: OUR AUTHORITY IN GOD

"Whatever you ask in my name, this I will do, that the Father may be glorified in the Son. If you ask me anything in my name, I will do it." John 14:13-14

Whereas the previous point was a giddy joy for me to write because I love being reminded of the healing God has given me through forgiving myself, this point is quite a bit more difficult. I want to take such added caution here because this subject of praying with specificity and expecting an answer can so easily be misconstrued and applied with selfish intentions. Quite honestly the fear of the Lord is on me as I write this, praying that you will hear only what His truth states and that nothing false will speak to you. Lord, speak Your truth with perfect clarity!

In a later section, we will go into more discussion on prayer generally speaking and its role in the daily life of a believer. However, at this point, I want to build up your confidence that prayer is a powerful tool given to us by God. It is a means of communication, yes, and a vital one to keep a relationship growing between a believer and God. It is also a manifestation of the power of God on our words and in our lives that we may see Him work in miraculous ways. When we pray for forgiveness, we must not be surprised that He forgives us and then forgets! We need to grow in believing that high-risk prayers like this are in line with the will of God.

It's a very easy thing to say a prayer that is pretty well generalized and then end with "...if it is Your will, Lord." This is how I prayed for much of my life because I was honestly too scared to pray something bold lest I upset God or give opportunity to others to disbelieve Him if He didn't answer in the way I wanted. Using this type of language was like a safety net. If He didn't "answer," then I supposed it wasn't His will. Safe enough.

One problem with this is that this is **not** how men and women of God prayed all throughout the Bible. This is **not** how Jesus prayed and taught His disciples to pray. Another problem is that this is watered-down and completely lacking in the boldness and confidence that is preached all throughout Scripture.

We must learn how to pray *within* God's will, *with* confidence, and *without* doubt! Doubt is a tool of the devil and he will use it at any chance he gets. Do not allow it! Through praying high-risk prayers, we exercise our authority in Christ to take action.

It's important to take a look at the difference between a high-risk, specific prayer and testing God. As with many things, it comes down to the heart of the person. In a high-risk prayer, you have an open heart that desperately seeks God's will.. His will is clear through confirmation from His Spirit, His Word, and godly counsel. There is peace that what you are asking for is what He wants. It is *not* a prayer offered with a selfish motivation or for personal gain. And, it is not to place conditions on the most holy God, to test Him or prove Him. *It is a thing done in obedience to God, not in defiance of Him.*

Read Hebrews 10:19-23. What do these verses reveal about the nature of our hearts before God and its role in our prayers?

It is His faithfulness and sacrifice that gives us the right to approach Him with confidence. How do the following verses show that we have the authority to pray specifically, expecting an answer?

Matthew 21:21-22

James 5:15-16

So how can we know God's will and know what to pray? Let's walk through John 14:1-17.

In verses 1-7, believers are encouraged to *believe* in God and not be troubled. So, here we see a blessed peace that comes from trusting in Almighty God, the Rock who will never waver from His firm stance.

In verses 8-11, Jesus *affirms the authority of the Father* that has been revealed *in* Him.

In verses 12-15, we are told to *ask anything in Jesus' name* and we can be confident that He will do it for the glory of the *Father through* the Son. Our asking is not to glorify us. And the authority from which we ask does not stem from anything we have done or who we are. It stems from Jesus alone.

And finally, in verses 16 and 17, we are told of the Holy Spirit, given to us to be our Guide until Jesus returns. We do not have to pray from our own wisdom. God Himself, through the Holy Spirit who dwells within every believer, *reveals to us* what to pray for and when. And we can be sure of the guidance of the Holy Spirit because that guidance will never contradict the established Word of God in our written Scriptures.

All of this hinges on an established relationship with God that allows us to be wholly familiar with the voice of the Lord. If we do not recognize His voice, we will not be able to follow His guidance.

God will always answer prayers offered to Him in humility. Often the answers come simply as a "yes," "no," or "not yet." But as you grow in your relationship with the Lord, and you are able to hear His voice with ever-growing clarity, these simple answers will often have more specifics. He is quite capable and willing to tell you not to drive down that road, eat that food, and likewise, which person to speak to, what to do around the house, or what errands to run. He does all this because He walks before us and with us and sets people in our paths that we could not possibly have known about.

High-risk prayers help us align faithfully with God's will and, therefore, bring us more into the identity of Christ as we trust God to guide our will and movements.

Read 1 John 3:21-24. What do these verses reveal about *why* He answers and *how* He abides in us to guide our prayers?

The very prayer of salvation that every believer prays is one amazing example of a high-risk prayer. It is an act of pure faith, selfless and trusting, putting your soul for eternity into the hand of Almighty God. It is also in line with His will for you because He has been seeking every person out who will come to know Him.

Another example that often gets a bad rap is the story of Gideon and the signs he requested from God. Before Gideon moved into a battle, he wanted to be absolutely certain that this was God's will and that God would guide him. Gideon's heart was not closed to God, making excuses. He was humble and seeking truth. And this is why God, in His graciousness, answered Gideon's requests for confirmation. He will answer you too when you approach him in humble confidence.

High-risk prayers are just that, risky, because of their specificity in asking for proof from God. And if we are to take up this challenge of seeking God's confirmation to our prayers, we had better know what to ask for. In order to know, we must set aside our own agendas and even our consciences because they are limited. We must seek His face and listen diligently for His voice. Once we have seen and heard, then we may ask with all boldness and confidence, certain that we will see our prayers answered.

4) GOD'S DIVINE HEALING

"Bless the Lord, O my soul, and forget not all his benefits, who forgives all your iniquity, who heals all your diseases..." Psalm 103:2-3

Do you believe God can heal you? When you or a loved one gets a cold, what is your first reaction? Not to discount the comfy blankets and chicken soup, but the first thing we must do is pray. Yet often, it is last, or often never even considered as an option, especially for those "common" ailments that will "go away on their own." First, let's consider that train of thought when compared to Psalm 139:14. *"I praise you, for I am fearfully and wonderfully made..."* We must never give our bodies the credit for healing themselves. All credit is due to the Lord because He is the Creator of our bodies in the first place. He made our blood to clot at a wound site. He made our skin to create new cells to replace the ones that were scratched off. He created our immune systems to fight off infections. So first, let's be adamant about giving Him credit, even and especially, on the so-called little ailments.

There are many sorts of healing. Yes, we usually think of physical healing first; but let's not forget that God also desires to heal our relationships with others, our thought lives, our emotions, and our spirits from attacks. Let's take a look at the different aspects of healing. As you consider each Scripture, be sure to ask yourself what is God's role, His action taken in providing for all the varying healing needs.

David describes the wonder of the created body in Psalm 139:14-16. God created our bodies to be good. But with the entrance of sin into the world, disease and the body's gradual breakdown from age came to be a part of our world's reality. What do the following verses reveal about *physical* healing?

Psalm 103:2-3

James 5:14-15

Forgiveness and reconciliation are desperately needed among families and within communities everywhere. We are designed to **need** each other and **serve** each other. What do the following verses reveal about *relational* healing?

Psalm 133:1-3

2 Corinthians 13:11

The thoughts we allow to replay in our minds–those things that we dwell on– can be either death or life to us. What do the following verses reveal about *mental* healing?

Romans 12:2

2 Corinthians 10:5

Being emotionally wounded can stem from abuse in our pasts or from sin. What do the following verses reveal about *emotional* healing?

Psalm 147:3

Hebrews 10:22

When sin entered the world, humanity was cut off from direct relationship with God. Spiritual death was immediate, the soul and flesh followed later. What do the following verses reveal about a person's state before knowing Jesus and the *spiritual* healing that comes from a relationship with Christ?

Isaiah 59:1-2

Isaiah 61:1-3

1 Peter 2:24

Our God is the God who *heals*. So how can we reconcile this truth with what appears to be unanswered prayers for healing, most specifically physical, such as in the case of chronic diseases? There are so many reasons God may have not to heal in the precise manner or timing that you may hope and pray for.

A Personal Note...

I have personally struggled with this very issue. I have Type 1 diabetes which is an irreversible form of diabetes. Believe me, I have prayed for healing of the instantaneous sort many times over. I've put out my prayer request to friends and family. Yet the years are passing, and I still have to test my blood sugar and take insulin. It can be frustrating that God hasn't answered my prayer like I expected He would. But I will tell you that He has been using even this frustrating disease day in and day out to heal other areas of my life. Diabetes has become a tool that God is using to heal me in deeper areas. He is concerned with my soul and that I am growing ever closer to Him. He's breaking my dependency on and idolatry of food. He's teaching me the benefit of building discipline in my life. He's working on breaking me of my bent towards a sedentary lifestyle. He's showing me that I need to lean on Him rather than worry and try to control everything. And He's helping me overcome my tendency towards self-pity.

Are you struggling with doubt regarding healing? *Take a few moments and ask God what He might be trying to show you even in these trying and frustrating times.* With God, every moment is a teachable one. And His plan truly is always the better one.

A beloved scripture is found in Jeremiah 29, verses 11-13, *"For I know the plans I have for you, declares the Lord, plans for welfare and not for evil, to give you a future and a hope. Then you will call upon me and come and pray to me, and I will hear you. You will seek me and find me, when you seek me with all your heart."* God clearly has a plan for everyone who calls on Him and seeks Him out.

But let's also remember that this wonderful promise was given to the Israelites as they were being led into a 70-year exile in Babylon. This promise was given *before* they went through a long trial, not at the end. I imagine God did this in order to give His people hope that would help them endure the long years of waiting and suffering. It was to keep them focused on Him.

How does Jeremiah 29:11-13 help you understand how your relationship with God relates to your purpose and identity?

God binds up the brokenhearted. He longs to set us free from the slavery of sin. This especially is an area where Satan will attack. He wants to keep you down and hurt. He wants you to remain wounded. But God has other plans if you will choose to accept them. He has great plans for you, and He has the ability to make you whole in order to carry out those plans.

5) SEEKING *FIRST* GOD'S KINGDOM

"But seek first the kingdom of God and his righteousness, and all these things will be added to you." Matthew 6:33

What sorts of things do you tend to focus on? More specifically, what claims your *first* attentions? In this section, I would like to explore with you what is meant by first seeking *"the kingdom of God and his righteousness."* What does that look like? I hope we can come to see in a very practical sense how having one focus in life will cover the multitude of distractions vying for our attention.

Let's take a quick look at the kingdom of God. This could easily be an entire series of sermons and teachings, but there is not space here for that unfortunately. The kingdom of God is most simply wherever God is King, wherever He is in charge and ordering His will to take place. So, the kingdom of God is in the eternal, spiritual sphere of Heaven, to be sure. But, it is also in the here and now. The kingdom of God is found within the body of Christ, in every believer who has made Jesus Lord of his or her life. It is not only relegated to the church. It is within the spirit of every person who has submitted his or her life to God. The kingdom of God is, has always been, and will forever continue to be.

What insights do the following verses offer about the nature of the kingdom of God?

1 Chronicles 29:11-12

Psalm 145:13

Romans 14:17

Hebrews 12:28-29

So, to seek the kingdom of God is to live a life in complete submission to the authority of God in your life. Have you handed over the control to Him completely, or are you still trying to be in charge of areas of your life?

What do the following verses reveal about worrying rather than relying on God?

Psalm 127:2

Matthew 6:25-27

We are also told to seek "his righteousness." Righteousness is basically "right doing"...doing the right thing according to the will of God. What do the following verses reveal about how to discern God's will?

Romans 12:1-2

What promises are given in the following verses about those who seek God's righteousness?

Psalm 5:12

Proverbs 10:6

Proverbs 11:28

1 Timothy 6:17

So, to take the ideas of Matthew 6:33 and flesh them out, if we as believers submit the entirety of our lives to God's authority and diligently seek out what is His will, we can be confident that He will provide for everything else– our physical, emotional, relational, mental, and spiritual needs. But we must put this *seeking* as first priority...not second or third or skipped over altogether. We will never be able to provide for our needs and wants like God can. By placing Him as our first priority, tied with no one and nothing else, we will be in better tune with His will and purposes. This will give us ears to hear Him. Listening and then walking in obedience to what He's telling us is key to living within God's will and experiencing His provision and blessing.

REFLECTION...

John 3:30 states, "He must increase, but I must decrease." To refresh and help these truths sink in, take a few moments and write down how each of the following actions allows God to increase in your life and you to decrease.

Repenting and receiving God's forgiveness of your sins (past, present and future)

Forgiving yourself

Praying with specificity and listening for God to respond

Seeking God as your Healer in every aspect of life, not merely physically

Submitting the entirety of your life to God's will and relying on Him to provide for every need

As He increases and you decrease, you continue to grow in taking on the identity of Christ in your life. Continue to allow Him to increase in every area. Hold nothing back from Him.

CHAPTER FIVE:

THE CYCLE OF RENEWAL

"Thus says the Lord: 'Stand by the roads, and look, and ask for the ancient paths, where the good way is; and walk in it, and find rest for your souls.'" Jeremiah 6:16

NOW COMPLETELY MELTED, the liquefied gold enters a cyclical process of refinement. The intense heat causes impurities within the raw gold to begin rising to the surface. Once the first fire has begun, and the impurities have started to rise, the next necessary step is to skim the surface clean. If the impurities are not skimmed from the top of the liquid gold, the impurities will fall and once again be a part of the gold. This skimming process happens many times as the fire boils the gold, so the Refiner can be sure to get every possible imperfection out of the gold.

This process relates intimately with our need to build into our lives discipline and time with the Lord. While our discussions in the previous chapter involved taking chances and getting out of our comfort zones, this section will discuss building lives that habitually involve God. Certain practices make this possible for our Refiner to skim time, and time again, the impurities out of our lives. Each time, as He skims away the darkness that rises up, we look more and more like Christ.

A Golden Truth:
As we stay liquid atop God's fire, He will skim impurities that rise up in our lives.

How does Proverbs 9:1-6 describe the Wisdom of God?

In Proverbs, we are offered an allegory that illustrates "Wisdom" and "Folly." Wisdom's ways are disciplined and productive. She calls out to those who pass by, *"Leave your simple ways and you will live; walk in the way of understanding." (Proverbs 9:6)* But Folly personifies a lack of discipline. She is seen sitting down as she throws out lies to all who pass her. *"The woman Folly is loud; she is undisciplined and without knowledge." (Proverbs 9:13)* Wisdom is one of the many precious gifts of God, which helps immensely in the lives of His children. There is a call to action in correspondence with a gain of understanding! We are called to "walk" in that "way of understanding." We cannot simply gain understanding and store it under our mattresses for a rainy day. **Gaining understanding demands action!**

Walking is a journey! It is continual. There may be times when your walk is more of a stroll; other times it resembles a sprint. But as long as you keep putting one foot in front of the other, you are walking and moving towards your purpose. In this section we'll take a look at how we can maintain ongoing spiritual renewal in our lives.

I want to be absolutely clear that you understand these tools are not meant to be interpreted as things to add to your to-do list to help you "earn" your salvation or so-called points with God.

Read Philippians 2:12-13. Think of the phrase *"work out your own salvation"* in terms of exercise. If you have received Christ as your Lord and Savior, you have been saved, and your eternity is secure in God's hands. But now you may not remain stagnant. You must stretch and grow and strengthen your faith and walk with God every day. Just like exercising is something that provides the most benefit when it is done with regularity, so it is in walking with God. You cannot meet with God at church on Sunday, live however you like throughout the week, and expect to grow in your walk with Him. Jesus must be your Lord on Tuesday and Friday and so forth…not only on Sunday. So, take steps with Him every day, and you will begin to see God moving you on your journey to an identity found in Him and a purpose beyond your imagination. Let's take a look at some of the key tools that will help us in our day-to-day walks with God.

1) FAMILIARITY WITH GOD'S WORD

"You are good and do good; teach me your statutes." Psalm 119:68

This entire chapter will spend a great deal of time looking at the role communication plays in our relationship with God. Just as in most marriages, you begin the covenantal relationship with a certain level of familiarity, so you do with God. It may just be as simple and basic as coming to a point where you truly accept that God exists and you need to know more about Him. With marriage, as time passes, husbands and wives grow in their familiarity with one another. And over the years, often the most precious things they share are the secrets that only they know, the quirks that they've allowed no one but their spouses to see. They understand better each year one another's character and interests and goals. So it is with our personal relationship with God. And the best source to help us grow more familiar with God, His character, interests, and goals is the Word of God, the Bible.

The Bible is not a testimony about amazing people or a list of do's and don'ts. It is a witness to every person about how God *interacts with* and *works through* imperfect people from the beginning of time and continuing today. By Him, we are created, forgiven, healed, and equipped to work out His will through our lives.

What do the following verses reveal about the role the Word of God plays in our lives?

Psalm 119:9-11

Psalm 119:114-115

Psalm 119:147-148

Philippians 2:15-16

Colossians 3:16-17

Whatever you expose yourself to affects you greatly. Marketers know this and capitalize on it constantly. They know that the more familiar you become with the brand they're advertising, the more likely you are to trust that brand and purchase their product.

Honestly ask yourself: How familiar am I with God's Word? Do I trust His Word more than anything or anyone else? Is the Bible my first source when I need wisdom?

Read the following verses and list the descriptors of the Word of God. How long does it last? How strong is it? What is it good for? How is it described?

Deuteronomy 8:2-7

Psalm 119:89-91

Psalm 119:160

2 Timothy 3:14-17

The Word of God is an immovable rock and foundation that can hold us securely in God's truth despite whatever else tries to sway us. It is also the primary offensive weapon we have against the enemy. What do the following verses show us about how the Word is used as a weapon?

Psalm 119:98

Ephesians 6:17

Whenever the enemy comes to attack us, he usually comes to accuse us. His plan to destroy us often utilizes lies that have a shred of truth mixed in so that, if we do not firmly know God's truth in His Word, we will be easily convinced in our minds that Satan is right. Knowing and applying God's Word makes us wise and proactive in protecting truth. This helps guide us in decision-making to do what aligns with God rather than what aligns with the enemy. Familiarity with the Bible also builds confidence in knowing who God is and who we are.

What do the following verses teach us about who God is and what He promises to those who love His Word?

Psalm 119:151

Psalm 119:165

Psalm 119:176

John 1:1-5, 14

Truth is truth. It is *not* as we are so often told, relative. And as you become familiar with God's truth expressed in His written Word, you will be better equipped to face every circumstance. You will also be enabled to discern right from wrong, ultimately understanding God's will in your life.

2) LISTENING & WAITING: INTIMACY WITH THE HOLY SPIRIT

"If you will diligently listen to the voice of the Lord your God, and do that which is right in his eyes, and give ear to his commandments and keep all his statutes I will put none of the diseases on you that I put on the Egyptians for I am the Lord, your healer." Exodus 15:26

Earlier in our study we took a look at God as our Equipper. He is faithful to provide the direction we need in life. He is an intimate companion, diligently walking with us each step along our journeys if we will simply allow Him entrance to our lives. One way, as we get familiar with His Word, to grow in our ability to discern His guidance is to be purposeful to listen to Him. We must shake off the noises that hinder us from hearing and create space to better hear His voice.

The Wisdom of God is personified in Proverbs, calling out for people to listen. Read Proverbs 1:23, 33 - 2:1-6. What promises are made in this passage to those who listen to the wisdom of God?

We are told that we must *incline* our hearts to hear Him...seeking His voice like a priceless treasure. Just as a matter of personal reflection, take a few moments and jot down what you consider priceless treasure. Is it a possession, a person, a skill, etc.? What do you value and place as highest priority? Does the way you invest your time confirm that? If, for example, you say you value your marriage as truly priceless treasure, do your actions agree with that statement?

If we will begin to seek the voice of the Lord as the most priceless treasure we could ever attain, God assures us that we will be equipped with understanding, security, and peace through His Spirit. So, how can we practically do that? How can we be so attentive and purposeful? First, we have to get rid of the noises that are distracting, whether they're physical noises or noises only in our own minds.

In Job 33:14 we see that *"God speaks in one way, and in two, though man does not perceive it."* What sort of things do you believe might be hindering you in your daily life from clearly hearing His voice?

Part of being purposeful to incline our hearts to hear the voice of the Lord means being willing to turn off the TV or shut off the music in the car...being willing to embrace the silence. Not that God can't or won't speak through a song or movie, because He can and will, but if you don't also create a space of silence in your day His voice will likely never become truly familiar to you. So even if He is trying to communicate through that song or movie or circumstance, you likely won't be able to hear Him if you aren't tuned in already.

Even our thoughts can often endlessly run, noisily bouncing in our mind. That's why we're told to *"take every thought captive to obey Christ." (2 Corinthians 10:5b)* We can choose to allow thoughts to become rooted in our minds, or we can choose to release them and speak God's truth, the Word, over any lies that are distracting and discouraging us from hearing Him. We are also charged with the responsibility to test everything against His truth. (1 Thessalonians 5:21) If what you hear does not align with the Word of God, release it. God is not a God of confusion. (1 Corinthians 14:3)

Embrace the silence and even take time to still your body. Give yourself permission to stop multitasking and truly focus on Him. He will meet you when you seek Him. He will answer you when you call.

What do the following verses reveal about God's response to us when we seek Him?

1 Chronicles 28:9

Proverbs 22:17-19

Jeremiah 29:13

Matthew 7:7-8

Colossians 3:1-4

Hebrews 11:6

Read Psalm 130:5-6. How do these verses help us understand the level of priority we need to place on waiting for God?

Jesus tells us in John 10 about the sheep and the shepherd as well as how trust and obedience are built and exhibited as the relationship grows. Read John 10:3-5. Are you listening to a stranger or are you listening to your Shepherd? Listen and follow. He will lead you to the green pastures and still waters. (Psalm 23)

3) PRAYER IS A TWO-WAY CONVERSATION

"When I told of my ways, you answered me; teach me your statutes."
Psalm 119:26

The verse just above is talking about prayer. But, if you look closely, I think you'll find that it doesn't look like the way prayer is often perceived. I have noticed, especially in our rushed Western culture that our practice of prayer tends to be more hastily spoken words and practically no time spent waiting for a response. People so often don't experience the value and the power of prayer simply because they refuse to wait on God to answer.

What is your current approach to prayer? How does waiting take place in your prayer life?

God spoke this universe into existence, and He is still speaking. He speaks to us through His creation, through circumstances, other people, activities, and also through silence. The ways to connect with God and experience His presence are countless. In this section, however, we will spend more time focused on hearing God during purposeful times of quiet and journaling. But I challenge you to consider the various ways that God speaks, and spend time asking Him to speak to you in many different ways. If you will simply wait on Him, He will meet you where you are, and you will see and hear how He responds.

It's a frustrating thing to pray and desperately desire to hear God's response, but only feel that your prayer hits the ceiling. One thing I've noticed about myself, and also about much of church culture and people in general, is that we're often in too much of a hurry. One thing I've experimented with over the past several years in my prayer time is to journal my prayers. Then I write a simple version of this question: "Lord, what do You want to speak to me today?" And then I sit in silence. I don't let my thoughts wander. I simply sit and listen with expectation that He will answer. And He always does! When I hear Him, I write down everything, even if it doesn't make complete sense. I like to distinguish what God's speaking to me from what I write, so I put what He says in brackets for future reference. I can't explain what it feels like to be able to read back what God has spoken directly to me over the previous weeks and months. Just as with any relationship, it builds more and more over time. And the more I communicate and wait to hear Him, the closer our relationship becomes. There is nothing magical about this method I've found useful. I don't have any more of a special ability to hear God speaking than you do. God speaks. He is always speaking. Will we tune in and take the time to listen?

What do the following verses reveal about our ability to have two-way conversations with God?

2 Corinthians 3:3-18

1 Thessalonians 4:9

James 4:8

When God first created humankind, His intent was to walk with us, talk with us and interact with us through every circumstance. This was the relationship He had with Adam and Eve. They had the opportunity to see His face and hear His voice. But their choice to sin and reject God built a wall between them and Him. What was holy and what was unholy could not commingle. Even in the Old Testament, though God had chosen the people of Israel to declare His glory to the nations, He still was separated from true intimacy with most people. Only a select few were able to hear His voice.

But the Lord, in His desire to have us close again, made a way for us to both talk with Him and hear from Him. Jesus demolished the wall separating us from God. He tore the veil so that once people receive Jesus as their Lord and Savior, they can return to the intimacy God intended all along. The way has been made for us! Now, we must jump the hurdles of our habits that we have walked in for so long. We have to trust that we are able to hear Him and make our schedules reflect the priority that the Lord is in our lives. As we read in James, as we draw near to God, He will draw near to us.

4) ACCOUNTABILITY & WISE COUNSEL

"Whoever walks with the wise becomes wise, but the companion of fools will suffer harm." Proverbs 13:20

Now, we can't stop at learning to hear the voice of God. If that were all that we needed to listen to, He wouldn't have designed the body of Christ, other believers to encourage and uplift us. One grossly miscalculated assumption in Christianity is that once we have accepted Christ, we do not need to mind anyone else. However, while we no longer need to seek out worldly advice, we most certainly do need to surround ourselves with other Christians who are wiser than us and who will tell it to us straight. Accountability is vital to maintaining our identities in Christ, as well as being effective members of the body of Christ. It is a positive reinforcement in those tough times and allows us to encourage one another to grow more and more.

A Personal Note...

When I was 19 and had just recommitted my life to Christ, I struggled enormously with self-doubt and the desire to find affirmation in relationships with the opposite sex. God, in His loving and humorous way, sent me a friend who was my opposite in just about every way. I'm 5'4"; she is nearly 6 feet tall. I hate playing team sports; she loves them! I'm soft-spoken, and she... well, she's not. She is three years older than I am, so only 22 when we met at our church's singles' group, and she was the new girl from California. Only the Lord knows why, but we became best friends. And on the only thing that mattered, we agreed: We loved God passionately and we each wanted to serve Him and learn to be more like Christ. I made a commitment to God to fast from dating for at least 6 months, and my friend knew about it. I remember distinctly one evening when we had just left a church service and were walking in the parking lot with a group of friends. One of the guys in our group was giving me a hug goodbye. But the hug lasted longer than her appropriated 2 seconds, and I was mortified to hear my friend yell at the top of her lungs from 100 feet away for him to let go of me. He was a sweet guy, loved Christ passionately, and hadn't meant anything by a 3.5 second hug, but that didn't matter to my friend. She was protecting my heart because I hadn't learned how to do that yet. She didn't care if she was annoying or embarrassing. She knew my weakness, and she was taking care of me. As the years have passed, I now see why God sent her my way. For several years, she was my very real, very loud protector. And during that time, I learned from her and most importantly from God how to protect my own heart.

Take a few moments and write down the names of the people in your life who are allowed to speak into you, even about the difficult subjects. Are they believers? Are they helping refine your godly character to reflect Christ? Have you given them permission to hold you accountable?

If you struggle to find a name to put down, take a minute to ask God why that might be. Do you tend to push others away when they offer any type of suggestion regarding things you may need to change? In order for those around us to feel empowered to speak into our lives, we must empower them in the first place. We must actively give people in the body of Christ access to our lives.

Do your closest friends share your belief in Christ? It is absolutely true and right that we be acquainted with unbelievers so that we can be a light of God in their lives. But it is unwise to have your closest friends be people who do not share your most central belief that Jesus is the Lord of your life.

Read 2 Corinthians 6:14-16. How do these verses reveal God's heart for our close relationships?

What do the following verses say about the results of our close friendships with unbelievers?

Proverbs 1:10-18

1 Corinthians 15:33-34

What promises are given in the following scriptures if we make godly friendships a priority?

Psalm 1:1-3

Proverbs 19:25

Proverbs 22:17-19a

Scripture is full of examples of wise counsel being given and received, as well as instances where foolish counsel was sought and followed. It's amazing to see how God uses wise counsel to keep His people on right paths and to guide them through their lives with their best interests in mind.

In Exodus 18:13-26, while the Israelites were wandering in the wilderness, Moses, as the leader, undertook to hear every complaint amongst the people. He was the only judge, and he carried the burden for over one million people–far too much for one man. But when his father-in-law, Jethro, saw what was taking place and the physical, mental, and emotional toll it was taking on Moses, he earnestly counseled another way: Delegate to wise men to share the burden. By following Jethro's advice, Moses was able to gain some rest and share his overwhelming responsibilities with others.

Read Exodus 18:13-26. How do the results of Moses following his own wisdom in judging alone compare with following Jethro's counsel?

Ask God if there are areas in your life where you are doing what you thought was best, but you are now feeling the effects of burnout. Ask for wise counsel on that area from a believer you trust, and see how God will show you His better way.

Read the following passages. What were the outcomes after godly counsel was given?

1 Samuel 20 (David and Jonathan)

2 Samuel 12:7-14 (David and Nathan)

Now, read 1 Samuel 28:3-19, and consider the difference here when King Saul unwisely sought the counsel of a medium, or sorcerer. Are there areas in your life where you are heeding unwise advice? Perhaps you may be gathering advice not only from people outside the body of Christ but also from mediums such as television, magazines, or the Internet. Do they agree with the Word and Spirit of God, or do they contradict?

Remember too, that as relational beings, we must be careful not to live in isolation, depending only upon ourselves. Yes, seek silence and solitude to hear the voice of God. Then, step out into trusted friendships full of accountability and wise counsel. Proverbs 18:1 says, *"Whoever isolates himself seeks his own desire; he breaks out against all sound judgment."* Are you seeking your own desire to the detriment of God's plan for you?

Who, other than God, do you listen to? Which people are your ears tuned into? Proverbs 27:17 tells us, *"Iron sharpens iron, and one man sharpens another."* Who has permission to sharpen you? If you can't think of anyone at present, then begin to ask God to reveal to you one or two people in your life that are Christ-followers that you can trust and be accountable to. He wants your best, and He will provide.

5) HE'S THE SOURCE; I'M RESOURCED

"Thus says God, the Lord, who created the heavens and stretched them out, who spread out the earth and what comes from it, who gives breath to the people on it and spirit to those who walk in it: 'I am the Lord; I have called you in righteousness; I will take you by the hand and keep you..." Isaiah 42:5-6a

So, now that we have begun prioritizing listening to God's Word, His Spirit, and the wise counsel from people He has placed in our lives, let's take a look at how we can put all of that into action. What are you *doing* with what you've heard from God and wise counsel?

God has created you with a particular set of resources. You have also acquired additional resources throughout the course of your life. Either way, the source is God, who both created you and provides you with everything. Now, what is a resource? Basically, it is an available asset. Resources all look very different, varying from person to person, and even within the same person varying from life season to life season. The bottom line is we have three main types of resources: our time, our talents, and our treasures.

OUR TIME...

Read Psalm 90:10-12. What does this passage reveal to us about our time and godly ways to handle our perspectives of time?

We each have been given the same number of hours in a day. But, it is up to us to wisely invest that time. *How* we use our time reveals the level of *willingness* we have to allow Jesus to be the true Lord of our lives. Moses objected at first to God's call on his life to demand the Israelites' release from Pharaoh because Moses was not gifted in speaking. But, as he chose to be willing to follow God's call, regardless of his discomfort, God provided a solution: Aaron, his brother, would be his spokesman until such a time that Moses grew in his ability. He may not have had the talent, but his willingness made up for that. God can work with any willing heart.

OUR TALENTS...

We, too, each have unique talents and abilities. Some are inherent giftings by God that just are. Others are abilities that have been honed and developed. There are three ways to handle a talent: ignore it, use it for yourself, or give it to God.

A Personal Note...

One of my talents is musical ability. I absolutely love to sing, play guitar, and write songs. I have used my talent in all three ways over the course of my life, with varied results. First, because I loved it so much, I used it for myself. I competed and greatly excelled. I honed my talent and invested immense amounts of time and money in it. And when I succeeded in my competitions, even though my lips said it was to God's glory, truthfully, I was puffed up with pride. In my mind, I did it. It was all about me. Then, after recommitting my life to Christ, I set aside my musical talent to focus on Him. I battled with ignoring my talent because I feared having to battle my pride again. There have also been seasons where this particular talent has been set aside because there have been other things going on in my life, seasons when I chose to redirect the time I would have devoted to honing my music. But, over the past couple of years, I have experienced something wonderful in giving my talent to God. Through some inexpensive group lessons, I learned to play the guitar well enough to lead worship in my small group. Pride is always before me, something I have to consistently place on the altar where things go to die and give my music back to God. But, through the constant battle, God has allowed me the honor of leading wonderful and wise women in worshipping God through music. He has trusted me with music because I keep giving it back to Him. And now I love and appreciate it more than I ever did when I did it for myself.

OUR TREASURES...

Treasures encompass all our material possessions, including our money. Treasure is not only the number next to the dollar sign in your bank account. It also includes the things you have in your house, as well as your house and everything else you have accumulated.

Take a few moments to read Exodus 35:4 through 36:7. How would you describe the attitude of the Israelites in their giving after God had called for the Tabernacle to be constructed? How does this compare with your attitude towards giving?

What do the following passages have to say about giving and the use of your money and possessions?

Matthew 6:19-21

Matthew 25:15-30

Acts 2:42-47

Just consider this honestly for a moment: If you had an "extra" hundred dollars in your pocket right now, knowing your needs were met, how would you spend it? What would you purchase? Would you share or give any of it away? Remember to be honest and take a hard look at yourself rather than give lip service to the "right" answer.

Considering the verse which says, *"For where your treasure is, there your heart will be also,"* (Matthew 6:21) how does your use of money and possessions reflect your heart's attitude?

Read Matthew 19:16-22. What is your understanding of what *treasure in heaven* actually means in practical terms? And, how do you understand it being stored up?

It's only been in recent months for me that I've finally grasped the reality of what Jesus was talking about in this passage. All this time, I'd thought that my good behavior was somehow my "treasure in heaven." But, now I understand that what God treasures most, that which is *His* heavenly treasure, is the *hearts of people*. If I am hoarding the time and abilities and possessions that God has lavished upon me for my own selfish pursuits, I do not have God's treasure as the center of my focus. I lay up treasure in heaven by being about the business of the Lord, by caring for the hearts of people, by spreading His Good News of salvation. In this way, by using what He has given me, I align my heart with His by agreeing that what is most important to me is what God most cares about.

Describe how heavenly treasure is different from earthly treasure? What does God care about, and, contrarily, what does the world care about?

Take a few moments and ask God to reveal to you the state of your own heart. Ask Him, "Where is my heart? How might I be pursuing *my* business rather than *Yours*?"

And let's remember that we don't have to source ourselves. God is the only Source we need! And once we have received from Him, let's put into action what we now know, and share our resources!

REFLECTION...

Read Romans 11:36 through 12:2.

Ask God to continue to transform your mind as you read His Word, listen for His Voice, follow His Spirit, surround yourself with wise counsel, and share the resources He has given you. I challenge you to memorize this passage so that it may be a continual reminder to focus on Him rather than be conformed to the mold of the world.

CHAPTER SIX

TURNING UP THE HEAT: SPIRITUAL WARFARE

"Beloved, do not be surprised at the fiery trial when it comes upon you to test you, as though something strange were happening to you. But rejoice insofar as you share Christ's sufferings, that you may also rejoice and be glad when his glory is revealed." 1 Peter 4:12-13

Now that the layers of impurities have been skimmed from the top, the Refiner begins a new cycle of purification. This time, the fire is hotter, the pot is cleaner and the intensity is higher. This intense heat brings the remaining imperfections and dark areas to the top to be exposed.

The first real "fire" took place in taking chances in our spiritual lives, in trying new things to experience God as He should be experienced: in relationship. This next "fire" is fueled by the heat of spiritual warfare. Denying its existence does not mean it doesn't exist. Spiritual warfare is the very real experience of any committed Christian. The evil one has no desire to see you succeed. So he'll turn the fire up in an attempt to force you to back down, force you to take steps backward. He wants you to get to a point of discomfort and fear and incapacity so that you will run away from the fiery trials. God, our Refiner, permits this fire because He knows our times of testing allow Him to be glorified and revealed. This chapter will look at the reality of spiritual warfare and steps towards conquering the fires of the evil one. Use the fires intended to push you further from Christ to, instead, draw you closer to Him.

A Golden Truth:
Even though the fire has gotten hotter, our Refiner equips us to emerge refined and victorious.

I do want to be very clear in beginning this section that while this is a subject we all need to be aware of, we must not place all our focus on "doing battle." I've gone down this road in the past and gone too far, which, rather than glorifying God, truly placed too much emphasis on Satan. So, I caution you to, yes, learn more about this reality, but only as you also grow closer to the Lord in your personal relationship, knowing that it is the Lord who assures your victory.

A Personal Note...

Even in the process of writing this book, I have undergone serious spiritual warfare. The evil one has no desire for me to share this message with other people. In fact, his goal is actually to keep the principles I have discussed here from taking place in my own life so that I feel so truly helpless and worthless, that I would give up on the project. How dare I, imperfect and hypocritical as I am, speak these words to others, and encourage others to work through these things when I myself have not yet perfected them? Yet, when I expressed this doubt to my husband, his response was simply and profoundly, "Obedience will not emerge from discipline. Rather, discipline will emerge out of obedience." Basically, if I obey the Lord's calling to write, to share this message God has placed on my heart for the past several years, then I will be forced into a situation that requires His help, His intervention. It will require me to surrender to Christ all my fears, all my imperfections, all my inadequacies...and it will result in something truly beautiful...a purer relationship with Christ, which is exactly what this book is about. I am choosing to sit atop the fire, trusting that through it all, through the pain and trials, I will be more purified and drawn ever closer to my God. The thoughts that have kept me away have included, and have not been limited to, the following: "The house is a mess, before I can do anything, it has to be put in order"... "I'm worthless and no message of any purpose could possibly come through me"... "I'm too busy"... "I'm too tired"... "I'm not in the mood to write." Or, I just flat out succumb to laziness and veg out in front of the TV. And it's all due to fear and sloth. Many times I've obeyed the dark whispers of the evil one instead of the steady guidance of the Lord.

What do you think of when you hear the words "spiritual warfare"? What does that mean to you, and how do you experience that in your life?

I've heard the following quote several times, and though I don't know the original person who spoke it, I greatly appreciated the bluntness...how it speaks to the reality of spiritual warfare: *"The enemy of our souls **does not** come to aggravate, exhaust and annoy."*

The truth is, that the enemy of our souls *actually* comes to *"**steal, kill, and destroy.**"* John 10:10 Just as God has a plan and a desire for each of our lives, so does the enemy. Whose plan will you agree with? What does that mean for your daily choices?

Read Genesis 4:3-8. Where did God tell Cain that "sin" was? What did "sin" desire?

What was the result of "sin's" victory here?

Earlier in this study, we looked at Wisdom personified. Here, we see Sin crouched in hiding at the door to Cain's heart! Sin didn't come in boldly and announce its presence. It stealthily waited for the opportune moment to steal Cain's relationship with God, to kill his brother, Abel, and to destroy Cain's entire life.

Praise God...we, as believers in Jesus Christ, have been equipped with both offensive *and* defensive weapons, with power and strength, with authority to fight the good fight and come out victorious! Let's get to know more of what all this looks like and means for our lives.

1) THE NATURE OF SPIRITUAL ATTACK

"Put on the whole armor of God, that you may be able to stand against the schemes of the devil. For we do not wrestle against flesh and blood, but against the rulers, against the authorities, against the cosmic powers over this present darkness, against the spiritual forces of evil in the heavenly realms." Ephesians 6:11-12

To get a picture of the "who" and the "what" behind spiritual attack, let's take a look at the very first spiritual attack in the Bible by venturing all the way back to the Garden of Eden.

Read Genesis 2:7 through Genesis 3:15.

The antagonist in this piece of the creation narrative is often translated as "serpent" or "snake." I've grown up having the image of a literal snake slithering up to Eve, being possessed by Satan and used to speak to her. But in comparing the original Hebrew word "*nachash*" with other instances in the Old Testament, it is often used as a figure of speech to describe someone who is cunning and in opposition to God's order. When this same word "*nachash*" is used in the Hebrew as a verb, it actually means "to enchant, fascinate, bewitch or of one having and using occult knowledge."3 In Isaiah 14:12, the enemy is called "Day Star" which is the Hebrew word "*helel*" meaning "Shining One."

I can much more easily see Eve being compelled to disobey the given order of Yahweh when faced with **an enchanting, bewitching, shining being of light** rather than the type of snake that we often conjure. So, whether you hold with the image of the serpent being literal or figurative, either interpretation highlights character qualities of this being that remind us of its mission to thwart the plans and purposes of Almighty God by perverted, cunning means.

The being that is often called "Satan," which means "adversary or opponent" is also called "accuser" and "enemy," among other descriptors. It's interesting to note that Satan, with the capital "S," is not a part of the original biblical text. It's a descriptive word, not a proper name. (Just as "God" is not God's proper name, but His position, it's helpful to remember this detail.) All of these types of descriptors refer to his position in reference to God. **He is *always* God's adversary, opponent, accuser, and enemy.** Hopefully, you are getting the picture that this is a being who stands in direct opposition to God as well as God's created order, including you and me. Now that we have an image of the "who" behind the attack, let's take a look at what an attack looks like.

Contrast the following groups of verses. What is Truth and what is the Lie?

Genesis 2:16-17 and Genesis 3:1

In Genesis 3:1, we see that Satan attempted to plant the seed of unbelief in Eve's heart by perverting God's Word. He took the truth and mixed it in with deception so that if you quickly gloss over it, it may appear to be accurate, but in reality, it is not at all what God said. When Eve repeated the truth to her tempter, he came back directly opposing God's Word by bringing into question God's intentions and appealing to Eve's pride and self-reliance.

It was then that the seed of unbelief took hold in Eve, and she turned her eyes to look at the forbidden fruit. This lust of her eyes led her to see the forbidden as good and delightful and desirable when in reality she was surrounded by countless fruit trees that God had provided which were hers to freely enjoy and were pleasant to the sight and good for food. (Genesis 2:9) **Satan got Eve to focus on the *desirability* of the thing she wasn't allowed to have and ignore the things that she was free to have.** He caused her to doubt God's pure intentions and perfect care for her. He led her to depend on her own knowledge rather than God's knowledge. And he encouraged pride to swell up in her that put her fully in charge of her life when that was never God's intention.

Does any of this seem familiar to your own life? Have you doubted God's intentions for good in your life? Have you been relying on your own knowledge rather than becoming dependent on God's? Have you looked at something you know is not good for you and desired it, or even partaken of that forbidden fruit?

Read John 10:10. What does this verse say is the ultimate goal of the enemy of God?

So, yes, this is something to be aware of! But, before we go down into the depths of fear and get overwhelmed, let's remember who Jesus is! Read John 10:10-11, 27-30.

Yes, there is an enemy with evil intentions. But let's remember who is our God! He is our Shepherd who protects us, guides us, mends our wounds, finds us when we're lost, and provides for every one of our needs! He came that we may have abundant life, not robbed and beaten lives! And no one, not even the devil, has the authority to snatch us out of God's secure hand! Take a few moments and re-read these last few verses we've discussed. Meditate more on the truth of God's care and promise than the present reality of spiritual attack.

2) MOTIVES OF THE ENEMY TO ATTACK

"Be sober-minded; be watchful. Your adversary the devil prowls around like a roaring lion, seeking someone to devour." 1 Peter 5:8

Years ago when I first wrote out the outline and general premise of this book, I wondered, "What sort of attack will come on me when I hit the 'spiritual warfare' chapter?" And, oh, what an attack it has been. It has been about ten months since I've even touched this book because the battle has been raging! In all that time, I've been hit with a period of depression, fear, doubt, anger, mental fog, and often a feeling of just being stuck. In this time, too, our family has faced multiple and often spontaneous out-of-town trips for my husband with me left alone with the kids for weeks, I've started my own blog alongside my husband in outreach ministry, we've endured the six-month process of becoming licensed as foster/adoptive parents, and received our first precious child to love on through the foster care system. It's been a busy time, yes, but I'm seeing, in looking back, that there *was* time to write. Often, I just allowed the attack to freeze me, to keep me so focused on my **feelings** that I couldn't focus on my **purpose** and on the **power** alive within me through the Holy Spirit!

So, why was I under attack? Why do I matter? This stay-at-home mom...this introvert...this shy woman who is happy reading a book or playing guitar alone...why? What threat am I?

Well...I just so happen to be a stay-at-home mom who is homeschooling with great intention. If we get nothing else done in a day, we will discuss Bible verses or have "devotional time" and discuss the things of God. We will prioritize developing character and cultivating hearts that love God and love people. That's a threat! And, yes, I tend to be on the quieter side, but God has grown a boldness in me to speak at many times when I previously wouldn't have. He's honing me with great purpose. And in this walk of obedience to the Lord's invitation to become foster parents, my territory exponentially multiplied in my opportunity to touch people's lives on a regular basis...hospital workers, CPS workers, CASA volunteers, attorneys, the child's biological parents and family, doctors and nurses and receptionists, government workers, people who see me holding a baby whose skin is darker than mine and ask questions, our family members who aren't believers and just don't understand why we do this...and on and on!

I'm a threat with a book in my hand because I only read books that honor God...that equip me to equip others, that inspire me to inspire others. I play guitar alone in order to practice so that I can lead worship in my small group. I write songs and pray that God touches hearts with them.

*Oh, yes, this simple mama is a huge threat. And my enemy knows it! I read the Word, speak the Word, teach the Word, sing the Word, breathe the Word, and share the Word. I am significant! And for so very long, in so many ways, the devil has whispered to me of my insignificance. I matter, and he tells me no one cares. He twists and turns the very things that I am made to do so that I fear them or avoid them. He is an accuser and the father of all lies! He knows I matter. He knows **you** matter!*

The battle starts before we even realize it, when we first wake up in the morning. Practically every decision we make benefits our walk with God and our reaffirmed identity in Him, or it reaffirms a downward slope into Satan's welcoming hands. When you seek to find your identity in Christ, be prepared to battle it out with the Evil One because you have just become a threat. Not only are you getting focused, but you will rub off on others and reveal the light to them too! He cannot afford for you to succeed.

Read Job 1:6-12. Why does God have such trust in Job's faithfulness?

What reasons does Satan give for Job's faithfulness?

Read Job 6:13-22. After such unbelievable, heart-wrenching circumstances, what is Job's response? Who was right about the source of Job's faithfulness?

How does that make Job a threat to the enemy?

Job mourned the loss of his children and wealth and the health of his own body. But he didn't turn his back on God. He did not allow his circumstances to dictate the direction of his heart and the purpose of his life.

What is the state of your faithfulness towards God? Are you a threat to the enemy? Why?

My battle is still going. And, from what I can see, as long as I'm breathing and seeking the Lord, it will continue to rage. I shouldn't worry when the battle is on. I should worry when I don't see any evidence of attack because that probably means I'm no longer considered a threat. But right now, in this moment, I will "...*Take up the whole armor of God, that [I] may be able to withstand in the evil day, and having done all, to stand firm." (Ephesians 6:13)* I declare this battle WON.

3) TESTING THE SPIRITS

"If you are not firm in faith, you will not be firm at all." Isaiah 7:9b

Not everything we hear is truth or should be acted upon. We have a great responsibility as Christ-followers to test everything that comes our way. If a spirit acknowledges Christ and aligns with the Word of God, then it is safe and wise to pursue. Logic is a God-given gift...*however*, whenever logic or sense goes against God's Word, we must defy logic. Look at Noah's age, Moses' age and circumstances. They defied logic and followed God's leading. But when something whispers in your ear about how ugly, unloved, or unworthy you are, remember, **this is a lie!**

Read Matthew 4:1-11. How did Satan try to tempt Jesus? What was Jesus' response?

I love that we have a God who wore our flesh and experienced our trials in His own body. Nothing we struggle with is foreign to Jesus. If He had to do battle, so will we. And who better can we look to in order to find a battle plan? Jesus knew the Word and knew His Father. Those facts alone gave Him the tools to defeat the devil. Those tools are what we need as well.

What do the following verses tell us about our enemy and how we need to prepare for him?

Ephesians 4:26-32

1 Peter 5:6-10

1 John 4:1-6

Our attitudes, behaviors, and abilities to discern are keys to successfully waging war on the devil. We simply cannot be victorious if we live in a defeated, pessimistic spirit. We cannot continue to live in sinful behaviors, treat others poorly, and expect victory. We cannot follow every whim without seeking to hear God's will on a matter and expect everything to work out in our favor.

What attitudes and behaviors may be standing in your way of waging a victorious battle right now?

Read Ephesians 6:10-18. Describe how each piece of the armor of God can be utilized in your life.

Belt of TRUTH

Breastplate of RIGHTEOUSNESS

Shoes READIED by PEACE

Shield of FAITH

Helmet of SALVATION

Sword of the SPIRIT, the WORD of God

PRAYER in the SPIRIT

Seek God's *truth*, not the swaying perspectives of the world. Put on His *righteousness*, not your own good works to depend on. Stand strong in the *peace* God freely gives. Hold up your *faith* before you, trusting that God is God. Know and wisely wield the *Word* of God. And *pray* in the Spirit, not only in the words your mind can understand, but also in the language of the Spirit, unceasingly throughout your day.

Also, do not think that you can battle on your own without other believers standing alongside you. Our brothers and sisters in Christ are there to encourage us...literally to build us up with courage, just as we are to do for them. It is God's design and purpose that we not have to stand alone.

Read Exodus 17:8-16. What is the problem Moses faced? What impact do Aaron and Hur have on the battle?

How are you allowing your believing friends to help "hold up your arms"? How are you helping others?

How do you begin your day? Do you begin on your own strength or do you begin by seeking God's?

4) IGNORING THE BATTLE WON'T MAKE IT DISAPPEAR

"Beloved, do not be surprised at the fiery trial when it comes upon you to test you, as though something strange were happening to you." 1 Peter 4:12

It is so easy to find escape in these present days. Television, internet, social media, email, over-planning, eating–just keeping busy so that your mind doesn't have to stop and ponder the deep things. When the heat gets turned up in your life, do you turn to escapism of some form? Or do you turn to God, your Strength?

As for me, I'm definitely guilty of seeking escapism. I cringe to think of the hours, days, weeks of my life wasted watching pointless television for the simple purpose of trying to block things out of the front of my mind. Because then I'd have to deal with them! I'm learning, however, that *coping* and *thriving* are very, very different things!

Read 1 Peter 4:1-2 and verses 12-19. What do the following key phrases/words speak to you about handling difficult times?

ARM YOURSELVES:

DO NOT BE SURPRISED:

REJOICE:

These verses alone speak so clearly about what we often don't want to hear: There WILL BE times of suffering. A life devoted to Christ is not a life guaranteed to be free of difficulties. To the contrary, as we live on this worldly planet, we are *simultaneously* citizens of God's heavenly kingdom. Two diametrically opposed worlds are certain to clash. And we will be caught in the middle. But we are not left without hope or resources. We have our battle armor...we have the Word of God...and most importantly, we have our Father God, fighting with us and for us.

Read Matthew 4:1-11. How do you see the stark contrast between Satan's kingdom mentality and that of God's kingdom?

How does Jesus do battle? What are His strategies?

Even Jesus stood on the spiritual battleground. If He was not immune from difficulties, how can we expect to put our heads in the sand of escapism and trust that things will just "work out okay"? Is there an area of your life that you have been ignoring out of fear of facing the certain battle? How can you come alongside God in this circumstance?

Take this example. If termites attack and infest your house, are you going to ignore them and hope they go away on their own? When you watch all around you start to crumble, and everything outside is starting to blend with what you keep inside for safety, are you going to just let it slide? What kind of steward are you if you don't protect the possessions and loved ones in your home simply because you did nothing?

The battle is raging…you are a part of it whether you accept it or not. You are not allowed to claim neutrality on this one. Whatever you do, you do it for the glory of God, of yourself, or of the Evil One. And whatever you do for your own glory, will never glorify God, but will, in the end, glorify Pride, which is a tool and the primary characteristic of Satan.

5) FAITH: BELIEVING THOUGH NOT SEEING

"Arise, shine, for your light has come and the glory of the Lord has risen upon you. For behold, darkness shall cover the earth, and thick darkness the peoples; but the Lord will arise upon you, and his glory will be seen upon you. And nations shall come to your light, and kings to the brightness of your rising." Isaiah 60:1-3

In all these trials, throughout this battle, we must remember the higher purpose. This is another opportunity for God to further purify us. Trials are the best way to refine us for His purpose in our lives, just as fire is the best way to lift impurities to the gold's surface.

Is God turning up the fire in your life? Is the Evil One working his hardest to kill, steal, and destroy? Of course he is…so this is a wonderful opportunity to turn Satan's evil purposes around for the glory of God. And in that, you will more greatly grasp hold of the identity of Christ. Remember back when we discussed high-risk prayers and our authority over Satan in Christ? In those times of tribulation, we must hold fast to this knowledge: Despite the lies and attacks, our faith is the substance of that which we hope for, and the Holy Spirit within us is evidence of our authority in Christ, which is a huge facet of our identities!

Let's start by taking a look at our already-defeated enemy. What do the following passages say about Satan's defeat?

Isaiah 14:12-15

Luke 10:17-20

Revelation 20:7-10

It is such an easy thing to feel overwhelmed by spiritual warfare. Fear places the focus on the enemy rather than on our victorious God. *There must be balance–**realistic awareness** of our enemy and his schemes while **standing firm** in the victory God has already assured us.*

What commands does God give us in the following verses?

Romans 16:19-20

1 Timothy 6:11-12

1 John 5:3-5

Read Daniel 7:9-14. How are God the Father and God the Son described here, and what confidence does that raise about God's sovereignty in all things, even in battle? Who is the "beast"? What happens to the "beast"?

What do the following passages say about God's promises to us during times of battle?

Psalm 23:4-5

Psalm 91

Ezekiel 34:22-31

1 John 5:18-21

When putting things in proper perspective, we can see that despite Satan's intent to steal, kill, and destroy, he is still defeated. His time of reign on this earth is over. When Christ shed His blood, *He took back the authority* over Earth that Adam handed over to Satan back in Genesis. But, persistent and delusional as ever, Satan continues to seek footholds in our lives, trying to convince us that our victories are not reality. He may be bigger than we are, more powerful and cunning. But, he is less than a pesky fly when compared to our majestic, sovereign, victorious God! When we are surrendered to God, we can trust in the victory He will bring in our lives. We can stand on the mountain, hands lifted high and see God defeating our enemies all around. Seek God! Do not seek strength within yourself to do battle. God has more than enough for everything you will need!

REFLECTION...

Read Daniel 11:32-36 and 12:1-13. Ask God to show you about the nature of your enemy, the devil, and his schemes. Ask Him to reveal to you the greater purposes of times of warfare and suffering and how they lead to the refinement of your identity in Christ. Seek God's wisdom, and ask for His understanding about the larger picture and your role in it.

CHAPTER SEVEN

PURIFIED: REFLECTING HIS IMAGE

"And we all with unveiled face, beholding the glory of the Lord, are being transformed into the same image from one degree of glory to another. For this comes from the Lord who is the Spirit."
2 Corinthians 3:18

AFTER BEING BROKEN, passed over the fires, and skimmed time and again by the Refiner, the liquid gold shimmers in purity. The Refiner knows His work has progressed to completion when, at last, He looks into the pot of gold and sees His own reflection as though in a mirror.

When we have been broken, and we have been put through the trials of fire, when we have been skimmed over and over again by the true Refiner, those dark places that were our own sinfulness have gone and what remains is pure. What remains is what God desires and what He has designed.

Now, a question arises: Does this level of purity come in this lifetime, or only in the next? I believe it is both. True and complete perfection can only happen when we pass from this imperfect world into a perfect heaven. However, God is our completion here on earth as well.

While the process of skimming and turning the fires back up time and again will continue throughout our lives here, God will give us those moments and seasons of pure, intimate communion with Him. That's what the purity we've been discussing here is. He longs to commune with us, and, in finding our identities in Him, this longing will grow in us as well. There is purity in this. And yes, now and again, impurities will be found and need to be lifted to the surfaces of our souls by the Refiner. But as time goes on, and we walk increasingly in relationship with God, these impurities will become fewer, and we will be further and further refined. We will look back and wonder how we were ever once that lump of raw gold–more blackened with impurities than lightened with gold. We will, in ever increasing measure, reflect His beauty, His love, and His Presence.

A Golden Truth:
Over time, and with increased intimacy with the Refiner, we begin to reflect His image and His Presence.

This entire study's purpose has been to highlight identity–allowing God to reveal His identity through us, His children, to the world that desperately needs an encounter with Him. One beautiful aspect of God's design is that His identity works *through* the individual facets He has placed in each person. He is not cloning exact copies of Himself. He has created us in splendor and beauty and with intricacies that are specific to each individual on the planet. Do not try to look like or act like the Christian next to you. That ignores God's purpose in the way He uniquely created you! Instead, let Him shine from within you, in all your individuality.

Grab a highlighter and skim through the book of Ephesians. Every time you read "in Him," "in Christ" or any other phrase that directly references being "in" Jesus, highlight that brief phrase. Then, go back and list out the promises for those phrases. *(For example, in Ephesians 1:7, I would highlight "in Him" and the promises would be that I have redemption through His blood and forgiveness for my trespasses.)* Over time, feel free to do this throughout the entire New Testament, reminding you of the many, many ways that Christ works in and through you, as well as the promises God gives.

Now, let's take a look at how *His* identity becomes *ours*!

1) DAY-TO-DAY FAITH

"...Being found in him, not having a righteousness of my own that comes from the law, but that which comes through faith in Christ, the righteousness from God that depends on faith..." Philippians 3:9

We've taken a look at faith through the lens of encountering battles within spiritual warfare. Now, let's look at faith in terms of our day-to-day life and what that means for our identities.

Of all sections, this seems to be the most difficult to get going. I've been racking my brain for fabulous examples of day-to-day living in an ongoing relationship with God, and I zoom in on all these "mighty" examples of huge faith. But what about the stay-at-home mom doing laundry and changing diapers? What about the worker who must clock in not a moment too late, after a morning consisting of a rushed breakfast and frustrating traffic? What about the retiree who feels bogged down by boredom or health concerns and longs to feel alive with purpose again? *Where's the life in the little things?*

In a new season here at my home, I've been able to enjoy a bit more quiet and ease in our routine's requirements of late. I've felt a bit guilty that things seem so easy right now, as though I should rush out and make a new commitment so things will get harder again. But God has brought to mind Ecclesiastes 3:9-13 and 5:18-20. The simple things like work, food and drink, and the possessions in our stewardship are meant to be enjoyed, all the while trusting that God is doing something beautiful, eternal, and mysterious within it all. It's an ongoing flow that necessitates a growth in our sensitivity to His voice. If we aren't sensitive to that, then all we will see before us is the work and food and drink. But if that sensitivity is allowed to thrive and expand, then we will see the work and food and drink as opportunities for God to minister.

Read the entire chapter of Hebrews 11. Choose a few of these saints and write down what some of their boring, mundane tasks of the day may have been.

Now, look at those same few you chose and jot down what great feat of faith they have been commended for in this passage.

Noah had a zoo's worth of manure to contend with every day during the flood. Moses had dusty feet and over a million people who whined to him daily. I don't know about you, but this encourages me with the diaper changes and potty training, the whining and the tantrums I face many days. These regular people dealt with ordinary struggles each day. And we look to them as examples of a faith that is alive and world-changing!

How do the ordinary tasks of these saints relate to your typical day? How can this encourage your soul?

Read Ruth 2:1-7, 23. What reality did Ruth face each day?

Read Ruth 2:8-13. What do you find in Boaz's comments to her that ties her daily tasks with her faith?

Just as Noah, Moses, Ruth, and other saints performed the ordinary tasks necessary for their survival, God was shining Himself through them. **The way they approached the menial jobs before them revealed not only their faith in God, but their ongoing, daily relationships with Him.** Yes, we look back, and we focus on Noah, saying he had great faith to obey God's voice, build an ark, and take part in God's plan. And we remember Moses' leadership and the miracles God performed through him. We recall how Ruth was chosen by God to be a part of the lineage of Jesus, the Messiah. And all this is absolutely true! But never forget that these were ordinary people, just like you and me, who reflected the image of God while performing the basest of tasks.

Read Zechariah 13:8-9. How are God's people refined and tested? And what do these verses reveal about our relationship with God and our identities?

2) PROVISION, PROTECTION & SECURITY

"...Charge them not to be haughty, nor to set their hopes on the uncertainty of riches, but on God, who richly provides us with everything to enjoy." 1 Timothy 6:17

In looking at faith as we live out our lives through Christ, we need to understand that all of our needs are met in God.

Read Philippians 2:12-13. What do these verses tell us about working out our salvation–both our responsibilities and God's?

Christ has saved us, and we also have responsibility to work out and exercise that salvation. But we are told that it is God who works in us, giving us strength to do what we must do. We don't have to do this in our own strength!

All of our needs are also met, and we are completely protected. Part of the problem we often have is simply a matter of perspective. In focusing on the "wants" of life we may not have, it's all too easy to neglect to notice and give thanks for all the needs that God has provided for us. Even more so, we often completely ignore the fact that many of our "wants" God denies us because they are not His best, or perhaps they may even be harmful.

Read 1 John 2:29-3:3. How is a father's perspective different from that of a child's?

Think of an example where a parent's larger, more mature perspective would save a child from danger. What would happen if the child could have had exactly what he or she wanted in that situation?

A Personal Note…

Recently we took our kids, ages 6 and 4, for their first dinner at a hibachi grill. My husband and I have been several times over the years, and we knew exactly what to expect: food cooked right in front of us with some humorous theatrics that included occasional, controlled fires. We knew the danger level was incredibly low and there was no need to be concerned. But as the cooking got underway, with the first fire the chef lit, our son leapt from his chair and took three or four steps backward to avoid being set on fire. His concern was genuine, and he was understandably cautious since he didn't really know what to expect. We'd given both kids some idea of what to anticipate, but it's different to see it in front of you.

Read Proverbs 20:7. This verse is written about a righteous earthly father and his children. But how might the principle in this verse be true as well for the children of God following in the path of their heavenly Father?

Anytime the Bible mentions walking along a path or in a certain way, I imagine a trail like you might find on a hike. There may be bumps…it may go uphill, then downhill…it might shift and swerve. Nevertheless, it's a clear path to follow. But, we can't set ourselves on autopilot and expect things to work out. We must pay close attention to the paths before us–step over the bumps, lean into the hills, and brace ourselves for the downslopes, turning our feet with the path. We have to remain aware of what God is doing and where He is directing us to go.

On either side of the path there are various distractions, dangers and temptations begging those on the path to detour. For those who stay steadfastly on the path, those dangers cannot pull them under. But, for those who succumb to the distractions, they face the consequences of having strayed. God is still there to reach out His hand and pull the lost up, to redirect them back to the path. But it's their choice to take His hand and turn their feet back to His way.

What do the following verses say about the provision God gives? What are our responsibilities towards Him?

Psalm 111:5

Isaiah 55:6-11

Matthew 6:9-15

1 Corinthians 10:12-14

We are God's children. His thoughts and ways are higher than ours. His perspective contains all of eternity. May we be wise enough to trust Him and listen!

3) DISCERNMENT & WISDOM

"The unfolding of your words gives light; it imparts understanding to the simple." Psalm 119:130

May I just take a moment to say that I *love* how our God equips! In this section, we will hone in on the *gifts* of the Spirit that God gives us–specifically discernment and wisdom. In the next section, we'll look at the *fruits* of the Spirit that emerge from our lives as we walk in our identities in Christ. God does not leave us in this world without tools. He knows exactly what we need and when we need it!

Let's start off by reading 1 Corinthians 12:4-11. List the nine *gifts* of the Spirit.

So, for quick review: Where do discernment and wisdom come from? Are they something we can conjure? (Yes, these are rhetorical questions! I hope the true source of discernment and wisdom is painfully obvious!)

It would be nice if we always knew exactly in which direction to go or which action to take, or even which words would be most suited to a given situation. However, we are not so perfect as to know these things from our own abilities. And, therefore, we oftentimes find it hard to grasp what is going on in our lives.

Earlier, I mentioned how I imagine walking on a pathway that goes between dangers and distractions of all kinds. One primary way we manage to stay on the path, out of the thorns or fall off the cliff is by growing in sensitivity to hearing God's guiding voice. The Spirit of God speaks continuously to us. We only need to stop and listen.

What things keep you from stopping and listening to God's voice? How do you feel when you *are* able to stop and listen?

The Spirit will tell us to go here or there. He may never give us the whole picture, but He'll always provide the next step, option, or a way out. If you were physically blind and you were having trouble finding a door, would you question the seeing friend who takes your arm and guides you step by step?

What do the following verses tell us about the Lord's guidance in our lives?

Psalm 73:23-28

Psalm 121:8

Isaiah 58:11

The apostle Paul did quite a bit of traveling for the sake of spreading the good news of Christ's salvation to the known world. Surely God would not have limits on where he could go, right? Wrong. For reasons beyond our understanding and certainly beyond Paul's, he was not allowed to enter Asia to minister. Instead he was sent to Macedonia.

Read Acts 16:6-10. Who stopped Paul and his companions? What was their response?

If Paul had heard the Spirit of God guiding him and had still decided to push through somehow–assuming it was physically possible–Paul not only would have missed out on the opportunities God had prepared for him in Macedonia (Keep reading chapter 16!), but he would've also missed out on walking in God's wisdom through obedience. He would've missed the blessing that follows obedience. He likely would have been distracted from God's purpose for his life and could have fallen into dangers or temptations with horrific consequences not only for him but also for those he'd neglected in Macedonia.

I've heard a quote many times in the past couple of years. Forgive me for not knowing its origin, but take a moment to consider the truth it has in your life: *"**People** stand on the other side of your **obedience**."*

Who may be standing on the other side of your obedience to God's calling on your life?

4) PEACE & JOY

"You have put more joy in my heart than they have when their grain and wine abound. In peace I will both lie down and sleep; for you alone, O Lord, make me dwell in safety." Psalm 4:7-8

So, our equipping God gives good gifts as tools to use for accomplishing His purpose in our lives. And, on top of that, He allows fruit to grow from His Spirit living within us! We do not have to create patience or kindness or joy. By allowing the Spirit to be our Guide and following Him, these fruits will be cultivated *by* God *in* us! Blessing follows obedience!

Read Galatians 5:22-23. List the nine *fruits* of the Spirit.

Have you ever read these verses and felt *condemned*, as though you "don't have these down yet"? Have you tried to work harder to love more, be more joyful, be more patient, and so forth? How did that go for you?

Yet another reason I love God is that He does not condemn! He *convicts* us which is a loving invitation back to His path. Condemnation comes from the devil and only serves to make us feel like failures. Condemnation never leads to a life that glorifies God. Conviction, on the other hand, absolutely will! *Condemnation **pushes** you down. Conviction **pulls** you up.*

Read Philippians 4:4-7. What benefits come to those who trust God and hand over their concerns to Him?

There is no need to waste time worrying. Rather, there is a beautiful promise of peace and abounding joy that comes from God! Even despite discouraging circumstances God pours out peace and joy.

Read Habakkuk 3:17-18. What discouraging circumstances did Habakkuk face?

How did he choose to handle those situations?

What abilities did God give Habakkuk in response to his faith?

Habakkuk knew his strength was very limited, so he gained true, limitless strength from the Lord. Despite famine in the land, he chose joy! God, in turn, made Habakkuk's steps secure and swift, just as a deer's, and He gave him victory over the challenges he faced.

What truths about peace and joy can you find in the following verses?

Isaiah 26:3

Isaiah 35:10

John 14:27

Colossians 3:15

It is faithless and false to think, "Everything will just work itself out." Contrary to this pervasive belief, God, the Creator, the Ultimate One has got it all handled. **He** will work it out. He has a plan and even His stupidity (if there was such a thing) is wiser than the wisest of humanity's wisdom.

When we rely on God to work through us, not only is our joy expanded, but also so is His. When God sees His children working towards their identities in Christ, He takes joy in them. He dances over them, sings over them...He treasures them. Just as loving parents adore their children no matter what choices in life they make, so does God. But how much *greater* is that joy when the Father sees wisdom being lived!

5) GOD'S UNCONDITIONAL LOVE

"I have loved you with an everlasting love; therefore I have continued my faithfulness to you." Jeremiah 31:3

Unconditional love...what might that look like? A dirty, sick baby who is helpless...would a good parent not pick her up and hold her and love her anyway? Despite the gallivanting of the prodigal son, did the father hesitate to lavish love on him?

Unconditional love is deeper than we can comprehend. Our closest, human equivalent is the love between family members, assuming you have had at least a semi-supportive familial environment. No matter how angry or hurt I am because of another family member, I love him or her regardless. God's love is *proven* by His sacrifice, by His continual desire to pull us closer to Him and by His ceaseless striving to purify us so that we may look just like His Son.

The golden mirror effect where Christ is reflected in our lives will be perfected finally when we arrive in Heaven. Then we'll better understand how every trial and pain along the way helped to purify us and bring us to this state of mirroring Christ and finding our sole identity in Him.

Read 1 John 4:9-16. What is love? And who is love?

Who does God abide in?

What is the evidence of God abiding in a person?

Read 1 Corinthians 13:1-13. Now, write this whole chapter out, but every time you see the word "love," instead, write the word "God." How does this alter or expand the way you understand love and the qualities of God?

This passage of scripture is another one I used to feel condemnation when reading. I felt I was missing the mark. And, yes, it is a fabulous illustration of what perfect love looks like. But we must remember that it is *not* our own ability to love that allows us to mirror these qualities! It is only God, working through us, that can create this kind of love.

What do the following verses reveal to you about God's perfect love?

Proverbs 10:12

John 15:13

2 Thessalonians 2:16-17

Let us not forget that "...*Neither death nor life, nor angels nor rulers, nor things present nor things to come, nor powers, nor height nor depth, nor anything else in all creation, will be able to separate us from the love of God in Christ Jesus our Lord." (Romans 8:38)*

That's a love we can rely on to guide us, to uplift us, to rescue us, to endure with us, to never leave us. The most beautiful thing of all that I have found, again, is that it is not up to us to muster up this kind of love. THAT is impossible. We just need to allow Him in, give Him access so that He can cultivate love through His Spirit residing in those who trust Jesus.

REFLECTION...

Let's go back to the original picture of refining gold. Read 1 Peter 1:3-7. Reflect on the progression of this verse when compared to the refining process we've walked through. What is the Holy Spirit telling you?

"Blessed be the God and Father of our Lord Jesus Christ!" **He is the Refiner!**

"...According to his great mercy, he has caused us to be born again..." **God has received us AS WE ARE–with bumps and bruises and impurities!**

"...To a living hope through the resurrection of Jesus Christ from the dead..." **He has taken our brokenness and given us hope!**

"...To an inheritance that is imperishable, undefiled, and unfading, kept in heaven for you..." **He has melted away our false identities and given us our true and everlasting identities in Him!**

"...Who by God's power are being guarded through faith for a salvation ready to be revealed in the last time..." **Our salvation is revealed in part by our faith and guarded by God who continues to skim impurities from our lives.**

"...In this you rejoice, though now for a little while, if necessary, you have been grieved by various trials..." **When the heat from trials and warfare turns up, we can rejoice in all that we know of God and in our relationships with Him!**

"...So that the tested genuineness of your faith--more precious than gold that perishes though it is tested by fire--may be found to result in praise and glory and honor at the revelation of Jesus Christ." **Our faith, having been tested and purified, will result in Jesus being reflected through our lives!**

IN CONCLUSION...

I am so incredibly humbled to have taken this walk with you. God is so good and has revealed Himself in so many priceless ways over the years as I've pieced this together. I pray that somehow you have been touched by God, that He has shown you how desperately He longs to intimately come alongside you as you live this life. I pray that He has shown you that your understanding of who you are is just a grain of sand in comparison to who He knows you to be. I pray that He will continue to work in your life and that you would allow Him to unceasingly refine you, skimming off impurities as long as you live so that when others look at you, they see Jesus. My ultimate prayer is that you have had a glimpse of finding your identity in your Lord, Jesus Christ. Thank you so much for walking with me on this journey! Be blessed!

ENDNOTES

CHAPTER 1:

1. Tozer, A.W., *The Pursuit of God*. Camp Hill: Wingspread Publishers, 2006. Print.

2. "Shorter Catechism." Westminster Shorter Catechism. June 13, 2013. *http://westminstershortercatechism.net/*.

CHAPTER 6:

3. "The Serpent of Genesis 3." The Olive Branch. December 25, 2010. June 13, 2013. *http://www.angelfire.com/nv/TheOliveBranch/append19.html*.

ABOUT THE AUTHOR...

COURTNEY COHEN has been actively involved in ministry since 2001 as a worship and small group leader. Alongside her husband, Steve, she has worked in apartment ministry, missions, and as a foster parent. Currently she partners with her husband as a co-founder and contributor to Now Found Ministries. The pathway towards finding her identity in Christ alone has given her a passion for helping others come to know the "I Am" as their closest Friend. You can peek into the rumblings of Courtney's mind at *IAm.NowFound.org* where she explores the very real Presence of God in beautiful, pain-staking, and even seemingly mundane moments.

For more information about Now Found and other resources, visit *NowFoundPublishing.com*.

Live, Create, and Share Your Story

Your story is powerful. Do you have a message you long to share with others, but aren't sure how to begin? Do you want to see lives changed, but writing isn't your strong suit? Do you long to see your heart's message in print, but are overwhelmed with the idea of becoming published? If so, we would be honored to serve and assist you.

At Now Found Publishing, we walk alongside authors through every step of the writing and publishing process. We provide services including proofreading, all levels of editing, coaching, cover design, and formatting while maintaining the heart of your message and your individual voice. Contact us at authors@nowfoundpublishing.com to live, create, and share your story.

For information on Now Found Publishing and our inspirational and life-changing resources, visit NowFoundPublishing.com.

Also by Courtney Cohen...

Available in paperback through:
Amazon & ChronicHealingBook.com
and in ebook on:
Nook, Kindle, iBooks and Google Play Books

The inTentional Mama
Now Available
through:
Amazon.com, Nook, Kindle, iBooks and Google Play Books

Coming Soon
to:
Amazon.com, Nook, Kindle, iBooks and Google Play Books.

more from the

inTentional series...
The inTentional You

CPSIA information can be obtained
at www.ICGtesting.com
Printed in the USA
LVOW13s1241140817
544948LV00021B/1265/P